THE DESIGNATED MENTAL
HEALTH LEAD PLANNER

By the same author

The Mental Health and Wellbeing Handbook for Schools
Transforming Mental Health Support on a Budget
Clare Erasmus
Foreword by Chris Edwards
ISBN 978 1 78592 481 1
eISBN 978 1 78450 869 2

Related titles

Mind Mechanics for Children
A Mental Health Toolbox with Activities and Lesson Plans for Ages 7–11
Sarah Rawsthorn
ISBN 978 1 78775 713 4
eISBN 978 1 78775 714 1

Mind Mechanics for Teens and Young Adults
A Mental Health Toolbox with Activities and Lesson Plans for Ages 11+
Sarah Rawsthorn
ISBN 978 1 78775 715 8
eISBN 978 1 78775 716 5

Supporting Staff Mental Health in Your School
Amy Sayer
Foreword by Pooky Knightsmith
ISBN 978 1 78775 463 8
eISBN 978 1 78775 464 5

The Mentally Healthy Schools Workbook
Practical Tips, Ideas, Action Plans and Worksheets for Making Meaningful Change
Pooky Knightsmith
Foreword by Norman Lamb
ISBN 978 1 78775 148 4
eISBN 978 1 78775 149 1

THE DESIGNATED MENTAL HEALTH LEAD PLANNER

A Guide and Checklist
for the School Year

CLARE ERASMUS

Jessica Kingsley Publishers
London and Philadelphia

First edition published in Great Britain in 2021 by Jessica Kingsley Publishers
An Hachette Company

4

Copyright © Clare Erasmus 2021

A CIP catalogue record for this title is available from the
British Library and the Library of Congress

ISBN 978 1 78775 544 4
eISBN 978 1 78775 545 1

Printed and bound by CPI Group (UK) Ltd, Croydon, CR0 4YY

Jessica Kingsley Publishers' policy is to use papers that are natural, renewable and recyclable products and made from wood grown in sustainable forests. The logging and manufacturing processes are expected to conform to the environmental regulations of the country of origin.

Jessica Kingsley Publishers
Carmelite House
50 Victoria Embankment
London EC4Y 0DZ

www.jkp.com

Acknowledgements

Sincere thanks go to Amy Sayer, Ceri Stokes, Caro Fenice, Dr Pooky Knightsmith, Hannah Wilson, Jamie Douglas, Marie Richards, Mike Armiger, Keri Haw, Rachel Bostwick, Dr Asha Patel, East to West, Dean Johnstone, Sue Webb, Michelle MacKinnon-Rae and Rachel Thomas for your support to me, as a DHML, and feedback during the drafting process. The people who checked the contents of this book are active in the field of education and mental health and currently leading the way as primary and secondary leads working in schools ranging from local authority and academy to independent school structures.

I must also acknowledge some great school leaders and inspirations who have taken the time to support me as a leader : Christalla Jamil, Patrick Ottley-O' Connor, James Hilton, Vivienne Porritt, Keziah Featherstone, Alison Kriel and the organization WomenEd for encouraging me to be 10% braver.

I also want to thank my family, Pete, Matthew and Rosie, for being extremely patient during the writing periods, and, of course, my fabulous head teacher, Chris Edwards, who has supported me every step of the way in trying to support our young people and building a whole-school culture of mental wellbeing. Finally, thanks also go to my fantastic publishers, editors and amazing production team for believing in my value and helping me put the role of the DMHL (designated mental health lead) into sharp focus for all aspiring DMHLs or those currently in post.

Contents

Introduction   II

Section 1: Briefs

1. Working with Human Resources and Teachers to Support Their Own Mental Wellbeing   17

2. Working with the Designated Safeguarding Lead and Supervision . . .   21

3. Working with the Governors and Looking at Policies and Governance   24

4. Working with the Pastoral Team   27

5. Working with Parents   30

6. Inputting Data and Tracking Outcomes   32

7. Working with the Mental Health Support Teams and External Agencies   33

8. Suggested Training for the Designated Mental Health Leads   37

9. Designated Mental Health Lead Self-Care and Wellbeing   40

Section 2: Planner

10. An Introduction to the Year Planner   43

11. Year Planner   45

12. Term Plans   49

1. Weekly Planner   62

    Conclusion   138

    National Awareness Days   141

    Recommended Reading List.   143

    Appendix 1: Staff Training: Awareness Raising, Teaching about Mental
    Health and Interventions   147

    Appendix 2: A–Z of Suggested Wellbeing Actions to Ensure Self-Care and
    Nurture   159

    Appendix 3: Suggested Outcomes for Measuring the Impact of
    Interventions   162

    Appendix 4: Pre-emptive Mental Health and Wellbeing Concern Flowchart   173

    Appendix 5: Individual Student Support Mental Wellbeing Plan   175

    Appendix 6: Engaging the Family in #familyMH5aday (Family Mental
    Health 5 a Day).   178

Introduction

In a Green Paper, the government has stated:

> We want every school and college to have a designated lead in mental health by 2025. The designated lead will be a trained member of staff who is responsible for the school's approach to mental health.[1]

This announcement is to be applauded.

The designated mental health lead (DMHL) is an essential leadership position that will ensure schools provide a mentally healthy climate for living and learning. The DMHL coordinates teams of teachers and support staff, including a nursing team and counsellors, working closely with the senior leadership team (SLT). It is the DMHL's role to coordinate the whole-school approach to mental wellbeing, overseeing an outstanding framework of response and supportive strategies in place for the emotional and mental wellbeing of both staff and students.

DMHLs need to be up to date with relevant mental health training and in a position to review the school's behaviour policy, curriculum and pastoral provisions. In addition, they work closely with the human resources (HR) manager, or the senior member of staff who is trained to do this staff support role, ensuring staff are supported with their own mental health and wellbeing. The DMHL also ensures parents are properly engaged, from awareness raising and destigmatizing mental health to lifestyle changes to individual programmes or interventions for children. A key aspect of the role is to set up structures so that supporting the identification of at-risk children exhibiting signs of mild to moderate mental health issues can be picked up early on.

I recognize that to begin with, due to staffing and finance issues, this role is generally absorbed along with other portfolios by possibly a middle or senior leader. For example, in primary schools and smaller schools the DMHL could be an additional role for the special educational needs coordinator (SENCo), or inclusion manager, or designated safeguarding lead (DSL), but we need to recognize that moving forward, in order for it to be given the gravitas it deserves and the time it

---

1   Department of Health and Department for Education (2017) *Transforming Children and Young People's Mental Health Provision: A Green Paper*. Cm 9523. London: HMSO. Available at: https://assets.publishing. service.gov.uk/government/uploads/system/uploads/attachment_data/file/664855/Transforming_ children_and_young_people_s_mental_health_provision.pdf

requires, this is a full-time role and should be given to someone who either sits on the SLT or works closely with them, so they can exercise the necessary changes required from strategy to policy.

A priority for schools right now is to appoint the right person to the role of DMHL. They need to ensure that DMHLs attend training that enables them to identify emerging mental health needs in children and young people, and that they are in a position to work with external agencies such as Child and Adolescent Mental Health Services (CAMHS) and the mental health support teams coming into schools.

I recommend the SLT and DMHL also read my first book, *The Mental Health and Wellbeing Handbook for Schools: Transforming Mental Health on a Budget*.[2] The aim of this book is to look at how a school can work creatively in tackling a whole-school culture of mental wellbeing and the essential first steps a school should take to ensure the structures are in place for the DMHL. It covers the need to:

- Research and audit the current wellbeing interventions in a school and whether they are commensurate with students' needs.

- Start at the top, with staff wellbeing.

- Establish a wellbeing zone for students to access.

- Set up peer mentoring.

- Set up interventions from extracurricular to one-to-one sessions of empathetic listening and signposting to internal and external resources.

- Oversee the teaching of mental health awareness lessons as part of personal, social, health and economic education (PSHE) delivery.

- Have a clear job description for the DMHL.

Appendix 1 of *The Mental Health and Wellbeing Handbook for Schools* covers the role and job description of the DMHL, which will be the beginning and focus for this book.

This book supports the DMHL by making suggestions on what to do on a term-by-term and week-by-week basis. Drawn from my real-life experiences as a currently working DMHL, it provides a yearly and termly planner, with 39 detailed weekly plans providing guidance and suggestions that will be relevant for all schools.

In this book you will also find short briefs (organized as chapters in Section 1) on:

---

2   Erasmus, C. (2019) *The Mental Health and Wellbeing Handbook for Schools: Transforming Mental Health on a Budget*. London: Jessica Kingsley Publishers.

- Working with the HR team and teachers to support their own mental wellbeing (Chapter 1).

- Working with the DSL, focusing on behaviour and safeguarding policies, mental health and wellbeing guidance documentation and customizing safeguarding software to include emotional and mental health categories (Chapter 2).

- Working with the governors and looking at policies and governance (Chapter 3).

- Working with the pastoral team and supporting staff who are in contact with children with mental health needs (Chapter 4).

- Working with parents (Chapter 5).

- Inputting data in school and tracking outcomes of interventions on specific students looking at academic or pastoral and mental wellbeing key performance indicators (Chapter 6).

- Working with the mental health support teams and external agencies (Chapter 7).

- Suggested training for the DMHL (Chapter 8).

- Prioritizing your own self-care and wellbeing as a DMHL, and getting the right supervision (Chapter 9).

How to use this book

This book is a weekly diary planner, and is intended to be used as a working document to support you in your role as a DMHL. In Section 2 you will find a year planner with six half-termly map overviews. Each half term will have six or seven key points that will map key strands from the yearly planner and include key national and seasonal events, as well as school events such as inset days (in-service training days) and assessment periods.

Each week will include:

- A clear purpose for the week.

- A to-do list (goals) and a space to tick off the item.

- Space to add your own to-do list.

- References to relevant resources, such as websites and documents, that may help you to deliver that week's aims.

- A place to reflect on the outcomes and impact of your actions on pupils' attainment and wellbeing – what is working well and what could be done better?

- A focus on self-care being an essential part of our daily routine, allowing you to record one thing you are grateful for that week and a mental wellbeing action.

- A place to record what you are currently reading or listening to (see also the Recommended Reading List at the end of the book).

- A short summary of the focus of the week, making it clear how the points on the to-do list will support the week's purpose and be valuable actions for you to take.

I recognize I have written the planner for the UK schools starting in September and ending in the summer, so you will note the weeks are aligned with seasonal events according to the English, Scottish, Welsh and Irish school calendar, but hopefully schools in other countries will be able to use aspects relevant to their own school calendar dates.

The yearly planner may seem a bit overwhelming at first as there is quite a lot packed into each week, and colleagues juggling this role with other leadership portfolios will feel the strain. My message is simple: one step at a time. Even if you do only one thing on the weekly list, you are moving in the right direction, and right now, that is what matters. The plan is you can go back to the yearly planner each year and build on your work in the next year, always putting the key performance indicators into your school development plan (SDP).

As the DMHL for your school, you need to have a clear understanding of what your role entails and a strategy to efficiently roll it out. I hope this DMHL planner will be an invaluable resource, offering a suggested focus for all DMHLs starting out tackling the 39 academic weeks.

BRIEFS

1

Working with Human Resources and Teachers to Support Their Own Mental Wellbeing

The Green Paper, *Transforming Children and Young People's Mental Health Provision*, states that part of the core role of the DMHL is having a whole-school approach to mental health and wellbeing that includes how staff themselves are supported with their own mental wellbeing.[1]

According to the Mental Health Foundation,[2] one in six adults experiences a common mental health problem, such as anxiety or depression, and one in five adults has considered taking their own life at some point. With statistics as high as this it is highly likely the head teacher or DMHL will come across a colleague with a mental health challenge.

It is not statutory but it is advisable for schools to have in place a staff mental health and wellbeing policy or guidance document that ensures a working environment in which staff mental wellbeing is supported and that enables staff to carry out their duties effectively. An example of such a policy is hosted on the Charlie Waller Memorial Trust[3] website, which has a real sample guide and downloadable appendices; there are also examples hosted on the Anna Freud website.[4] A policy should encourage staff to accept responsibility for their own mental health and help build a culture in the school in which mental health and wellbeing is taken seriously and in which staff are supported in order that they may seek any help they need.

---

1   Department of Health and Department for Education (2017) *Transforming Children and Young People's Mental Health Provision: A Green Paper*. Cm 9523. London: HMSO, p.19. Available at: https://assets. publishing. service.gov.uk/government/uploads/system/uploads/attachment_data/file/664855/ Transforming_children_and_young_people_s_mental_health_provision.pdf
2   Mental Health Foundation (2016) *Fundamental Facts about Mental Health 2016*. Available at: www. mentalhealth.org.uk/publications/fundamental-facts-about-mental-health-2016
3   Charlie Waller Memorial Trust (no date) 'Mental health policy and plan.' Available at: https:// charliewaller.org/what-we-do/for-employers/writing-a-mental-health-policy
4   See, for example, Garland, L., Linehan, T., Merrett, N., Smith, J. and Payne, C. (2018) *Ten Steps Towards School Staff Wellbeing*. London: Anna Freud National Centre for Children and Families. Available at: www.annafreud.org/media/8459/school-staff-wellbeing-report-final.pdf; see also www.annafreud.org/ insights/news/2018/11/ten-steps-towards-school-staff-wellbeing-resource-launched

The DMHL, working closely with the head teacher and HR manager, or SLT staff member with HR training, should roll out a programme to support staff that involves:

- Changing attitudes:
  - Destigmatizing mental health and raising awareness that it is okay to not be okay and that there is no shame in talking about how we are feeling.
  - Raising awareness on what the early warning signs are, such as an increase in unexplained absences, changes in behaviour or performance or erratic displays of emotion.

- Changing culture:
  - Make opportunities available in the school for staff to have that first conversation about their mental health. This might include ensuring line managers don't just talk about performance but also check in with the staff they line manage, encouraging colleagues to adopt a culture of care, looking out for the signs with their colleagues, and checking in with anyone they are concerned about.
  - Having the first item on every line management meeting: 'Wellbeing: How is your wellbeing?' And then really listening and avoiding responses that make the colleague feel like everyone else is doing fine and it's just them.
  - Understanding that when colleagues say, 'No, I can't', it could be about self-preservation and *putting on your own oxygen mask first*, rather than them being difficult or un-cooperative or a sign of disorganized management.

- Listening to staff voices:
  - Conducting staff surveys to gauge the mental wellbeing barometer of school staff and preparing a 'You said, we did' response to show staff that the SLT is listening.

- Changing structures:
  - Encouraging mental wellbeing champions and secret buddy systems to encourage teamwork and to ensure everyone is made to feel valued.
  - Making available the position of an HR manager on the staff body who staff can go to and disclose their personal problems that they are facing that might be resulting in mental health challenges. The HR manager

will be able to ask about what workplace triggers might affect them (including work pressures or relationships with colleagues) and what support or adjustments the school can put in place to support them. Amy Sayer's book, *Supporting Staff Mental Health in Your School*,[5] is an important reference here as it gives insightful case studies and examples of support plans and reasonable adjustments a school can make to support their staff, and I strongly urge DMHLs to read it.

- Signposting help:

    - Signposting help for colleagues is vital. This might include help from Education Support,[6] which offers information, counselling and a range of resources on managing stress for school and college staff. There is also a prolific amount of online support from organizations and charities such as Mind.[7]

- Understanding mental health and legal rights:

    - A mental health difficulty can qualify as a disability under the Equality Act 2010. This means that a member of staff has the legal right to request reasonable adjustments to be made to their work routine, their work environment or how they do their job.[8]

    - Together with the head teacher and the HR manager and DMHL supporting, the school can make reasonable adjustments – from allowing time off for medical appointments, to reducing their timetable, identifying the triggers in a school day and, where possible, removing them, allowing the member of staff to have opportunities to talk and check in with the HR manager on their progress.

    - Mind has also produced some very good advice for school leaders on how to support their teams at work.[9] This could be very beneficial continuing professional development (CPD) for all middle leaders and senior leadership staff on supporting their teams.

- Offering supervision for those on the front line:

    - Providing supervision for staff who work with students with complex mental health issues is also becoming an area that the DMHL will

---

5   Sayer, A. (2020) *Supporting Staff Mental Health in Your School*. London: Jessica Kingsley Publishers.
6   www.educationsupport.org.uk
7   www.mind.org.uk
8   Anna Freud National Centre for Children and Families (no date) 'Supporting a member of staff with mental health difficulties.' Available at: www.mentallyhealthyschools.org.uk/whole-school-approach/supporting-a-member-of-staff-with-mental-health-difficulties
9   www.mind.org.uk/workplace/mental-health-at-work/taking-care-of-your-staff/useful-resources

need for themselves and to provide for the pastoral team who work closely with some of these cases. The emotional impact of working with students who have mental health needs can be very stressful. In the Anna Freud National Centre for Children and Families' *Ten Steps Towards School Staff Wellbeing* it states that supervision provides an opportunity to think about the needs of pupils or to consider an area of work the staff member is finding especially challenging, and it can reduce the sense of being alone in dealing with a problem.[10] Supervision can be conducted by a qualified coach supervisor or a clinical mental health expert where the service is contracted in. In some schools the DMHL may well be the one trained to offer the supervision to fellow staff, in which case the DMHL and DSL should receive supervision from a clinical expert where it is contracted in from an external agency (see Chapter 2 for more details).

- Role modelling staff wellbeing:

  - Finally, school leaders and managers should, where possible, role model a healthy life–work balance and encourage a culture of mental wellbeing. This can include no expectations for staff to work at weekends; a moratorium on emails in the evenings and weekends; modelling a good life–work balance; and encouraging staff to focus on the five steps to mental wellbeing cited on the NHS (National Health Service) website – connecting with others; being physically active; learning new skills; giving to others; and being mindful.[11]

10 Garland, L., Linehan, T., Merrett, N., Smith, J. and Payne, C. (no date) *Ten Steps Towards School Staff Wellbeing*. London: Anna Freud National Centre for Children and Families. Available at: www.annafreud.org/media/8459/school-staff-wellbeing-report-final.pdf

11 NHS (no date) '5 steps to mental wellbeing.' Available at: www.nhs.uk/conditions/stress-anxiety-depression/improve-mental-wellbeing

2

Working with the Designated Safeguarding Lead and Supervision

The DSL is a senior member of staff from the SLT who takes responsibility for safeguarding and child protection. They are given time, funding, training and resources to provide advice and support to other staff on child welfare and child protection matters, and take part in strategy discussions and interagency meetings. They are expected to:

- Manage referrals for suspected cases of abuse or radicalization or refer cases where a crime may have been committed.

- Work with others, including safeguarding partners, the police and case managers, and to support and liaise with staff on matters of safety and safeguarding and when to make a referral to the relevant agencies.

- Raise awareness of child protection policies and ensure there are training opportunities for staff on safeguarding arrangements.

- Ensure all child protection files are kept up to date and all interventions recorded, including outcomes.

It is essential that staff are aware of their responsibilities, as set out in the statutory guidance (Part 1 of *Keeping Children Safe in Education*[1] and also in *Working Together to Safeguard Children*[2]). It might be the case that a mental health problem that a pupil is facing is due to the pupil suffering, or at risk of suffering, abuse, neglect or exploitation. If staff have a mental health concern, due diligence should be followed and action should be taken, following the school's child protection policy.[3]

In our school I worked closely with the DSL on the following:

---

1   Department for Education (2020) *Keeping Children Safe in Education: Statutory Guidance for Schools and Colleges*. London: HMSO. Available at: https://assets.publishing.service.gov.uk/government/uploads/system/uploads/attachment_data/file/912592/Keeping_children_safe_in_education_Sep_2020.pdf

2   Department for Education (2015) *Working Together to Safeguard Children: Statutory Guidance on Inter-Agency Working to Safeguard and Promote the Welfare of Children*. [Updated in 2020.] Available at: www.gov.uk/government/publications/working-together-to-safeguard-children--2

3   Department for Education (2018) *Mental Health and Behaviour in Schools*. London: HMSO. Available at: https://assets.publishing.service.gov.uk/government/uploads/system/uploads/attachment_data/file/755135/Mental_health_and_behaviour_in_schools__.pdf

- Ensuring that the mental health and wellbeing guidance document was not something separate to the school's safeguarding policy or behaviour policy but rather in sync with existing policies, ensuring it was also consistent with the school's duties under the Equality Act 2010. Instead of making a separate safeguarding referral about a student's mental health to the DMHL, we ensured *all safeguarding concerns* were made to the DSL team in the first instance. It was then that the *DSL team* would triage and read the referral, and if it was deemed a mental health concern, it would be referred on to the DMHL and the mental health first aider (MHFA) for further intervention.

- Ensuring the software we used to record safeguarding incidents was customized to reflect a range of emotional mental health challenges, such as phobias, anxiety disorders and depression (emotional disorders); or behavioural challenges, such as stealing, defiance, aggression and anti-social behaviour (conduct disorders); or disturbance of activity and attention (hyperkinetic disorders). This meant staff who were recording the incident were able to be as specific as possible about what they had observed or the disclosure that had been made to them.

- Having an oversight role to ensure mental health was reflected in the curriculum and it was part of our pre-emptive and proactive whole-school culture on mental health and wellbeing. This included teaching students about mental health illnesses and lifestyle choices for positive mental wellbeing through the curriculum, thus equipping students to be resilient so that they could manage the normal stress of life effectively.

- Setting up physical structures in the school for student support so they would know where to go for support (self-referral), when to go, and what to expect when they feel the need to talk or disclose something.

- Engaging with parents supporting the identification of at-risk children where there are clear links to mental health.

- Coordinating the mental health needs of students and overseeing the outcomes of interventions on students' education and wellbeing.

- Supporting staff in contact with students with mental health needs.

I would suggest meeting regularly with the DSL to discuss the above to ensure you work collaboratively and are making best use of time, staffing and resources.

Finally, supervision for the DMHL and DSL for their own wellbeing needs important attention. There is an emotional strain that comes with managing the kind of safeguarding and mental health issues that arise at schools. Supervision can reduce the sense of being alone in dealing with a problem. It can be conducted by a qualified coach, supervisor or a clinical mental health expert where the service is contracted in. In some schools the DMHL may well be the one trained to offer the supervision to fellow staff, and then the DMHL and DSL receive supervision from a clinical expert where it is contracted in from an external agency. This is an area of support that should not be overlooked for the DMHL and DSL.

There are a number of ways you can get supervision in school and externally. I am particularly impressed with the National Centre for Supervision in Education that not only offers supervision to teachers but also a Supervision in Education Award to allow your school to be recognized as an educational provider that understands the impact of supporting children's increasing mental health needs by creating a culture of supervision across the organization.

The National Centre for Supervision in Education[4] focuses on providing support and training for teachers and educators whose role involves supporting children and young people with issues affecting their wellbeing and mental health such as stress or anxiety. It aims to improve children and young people's educational experience by helping schools and educational providers embed an improved culture of support and resilience within their staff community. The initiative is led by the Carnegie School of Education in development with Talking Heads, and aims to address the increasing demands being placed on all staff members within educational settings. This comes at a time when other services that have traditionally supported schools are being reduced. Supervision holds the child or young person at the centre of the supervision working alliance, but also meets the support needs of the educator, through a confidential, regular supervision space for reflection, enquiry and challenge. The National Centre for Supervision in Education Hub has developed an Award to allow schools to be recognized as educational providers that understand the impact of supporting children's increasing mental health needs by creating a culture of supervision across the organization, developing an environment where staff are supported with maintaining their emotional wellbeing, enabling them to provide a supportive learning experience for the children and young people they educate.

All of the National Centre for Supervision in Education Hub supervisors have been through a recruitment and selection process.

All supervisors are registered with a professional membership body such as the Health and Care Professions Council (HCPC), UK Council for Psychotherapy (UKCP), British Psychological Society (BPS) and British Association for Counselling and Psychotherapy (BACP), or they have an accredited qualification.

4   www.leedsbeckett.ac.uk/carnegie-school-of-education/national-hub-for-supervision-in-education

3

Working with the Governors and Looking at Policies and Governance

An effective governing body can play a very important role in helping a school set up a culture of mental wellbeing. Some schools are appointing a wellbeing governor and, by doing this, the governing board is showing its commitment to supporting the mental health and wellbeing of all stakeholders in the school.

It would be the DMHL's role to work closely with the wellbeing governor in establishing a robust mental health and wellbeing culture in the school, which also ensures clarity in the process and provisions.

Governing bodies have a duty[1] to promote wellbeing. In schools in England, this is through promoting:[2]

- Physical and mental health, and emotional wellbeing.

- Protection from harm and neglect.

- Education, training and recreation.

- The contribution children make to society.

- Social and economic wellbeing.

Governors and trustees can support pupil mental health and wellbeing by working with the DMHL and SLT to:

- Oversee the implementation of student and staff mental health and wellbeing policies or guidance documents and to review these on an annual basis. Updating and making changes benefits the key stakeholders.

- Ensure all stakeholders – staff, students, parents and carers – are clear about the strategic mental health and wellbeing vision of the school, what is available to support them, and processes they can follow. They should oversee with the DMHL any training that is required to ensure the vision is enabled.

---

1   Education and Inspections Act 2006, see www.legislation.gov.uk/ukpga/2006/40/contents
2   Children Act 2004, see www.legislation.gov.uk/ukpga/2004/31/section/10

- Conduct surveys and focus groups and get feedback from the stakeholders and work with the DMHL in refining the strategic focus based on the feedback.

- Oversee the roll-out of teaching about mental health and wellbeing in the curriculum that will enable the students to make informed choices about supporting their own and others' emotional wellbeing, thereby making a positive contribution to society.

- Ensure that as a school the understanding is that like physical health, we all have mental health and a duty to check in with each other, look out for the signs and ensure colleagues and peers are supported and signposted to where there is help.

More can be read from the National Governance Association,[3] where Dr Pooky Knightsmith explains the critical contribution the governing body can play in supporting the mental health of students in a school.

We had a wonderful wellbeing governor in our school who helped mastermind the physical structures around the school, from the setting up of the #wellbeingsquare (the wellbeing zone, the student area for lunchtime support) to the staff mental wellbeing room. She was able to help us access local community deals and as she was also an artist was able to give up her time to inspire the physical look. She was a real wellbeing warrior and her passion definitely inspired and supported me as the DMHL in helping realize the school's strategic vision.

Regarding training for the governor in the creation of the wellbeing governor role, they can follow a Mental Health and Wellbeing Lead Governor Status E-Module,[4] which is delivered by the Carnegie Centre of Excellence for Mental Health in Schools Professional Learning Programme. The multiple choice assessment will take a maximum of one hour to complete and the programme is delivered online and can be started at any time. Completing the E-Module will give the person the status of being a Carnegie Mental Health and Wellbeing Lead Governor.

Finally, if the school budget allows, the DMHL might want to negotiate with the governing body to use an all-inclusive online platform that will help the DMHL to assess, manage and receive training and have access to a wealth of online resource and consultation support from mental health clinical experts. I have used EduPod and have found its wealth of online support features, ongoing training and webinars and online support from experts extremely helpful.

---

3   Knightsmith, P. (no date) 'Promoting positive mental health.' National Governance Association. Available at: www.nga.org.uk/Knowledge-Centre/Pupil-success-and-wellbeing/Pupil-wellbeing/Mental-health/Promoting-positive-mental-health.aspx
4   See www.leedsbeckett.ac.uk/-/media/files/school-of-education/professional-learning-programmes-2020.pdf

Developed by Innovating Minds CIC, EduPod[5] is the first online platform for mental health leads. It is a new way for mental health leads to plan, manage and evaluate their journey to creating happy and mentally healthy environments for the whole-school community. As a one-stop-shop, it enables individual schools and academies to monitor and evaluate their whole-school approach strategy, conduct surveys, and to access professional mental health resources, recommended actions and consultation support from professionals.

EduPod offers:[6]

- An evidence-based audit tool that will enable you to self-assess your journey to creating a whole-school approach.

- Access to pre-generated surveys that will allow you to capture feedback from the school community. EduPod will also analyse the data for you.

- The ability to record and measure the impact of implementing a whole-school approach.

- Access to over 100 resources to help you implement your strategy by learning from schools and experts within the field of mental health.

- Guidance from a team of experts from Innovating Minds and the EduPod community.

- An accreditation scheme that rewards the journey from commitment to excelling in the implementation.

5   www.myedupod.com
6   Find out more at www.myedupod.com, or email info@innovatingmindscic.com

4

Working with the Pastoral Team

The pastoral team can be made up of a mixture of non-teaching and teaching staff who can have a range of titles, from pastoral managers, heads of year and heads of houses, MHFAs, family link support workers and pastoral supporting staff. These members of staff will often be on the front line dealing with young people and their behaviour, young people who are struggling in lessons or break times, and they may be in frequent contact with children with mental health challenges.

The Department for Education guidance document, *Mental Health and Behaviour in Schools*, states:

> Schools need to be alert to how mental health problems can underpin behaviour issues in order to support pupils effectively, working with external support where needed. They also need to be aware of their duties under the Equality Act 2010, recognizing that some mental health issues will meet the definition of disability.[1]

A school's pastoral support plan, including its behaviour policy, should form part of a whole-school approach to mental health and wellbeing. It is not compulsory for schools to have a mental health and wellbeing policy in place, but it is advisable for all schools to have a mental health and wellbeing guidance document. This will give the pastoral support team and educators some clarity on processes when the behavioural issues might be a result of mental health needs. The school needs to have a clear system and processes in place for identifying possible mental health challenges, and then a clear internal referral system that ensures support. These processes should ideally be clearly documented in either the mental health policy or guidance document. In Appendix 4 to this book you will see a flowchart of the referral process in place in a school where I work.

It is advisable that the DMHL works closely with the pastoral team to help support these middle leaders and support staff in identifying young people whose behaviour issues might be as a result of mental health needs. I would suggest meeting regularly with different members of the pastoral support team, sometimes

---

[1] Department for Education (2018) *Mental Health and Behaviour in Schools*. London: HMSO, p.5. Available at: https://assets.publishing.service.gov.uk/government/uploads/system/uploads/attachment_data/file/755135/Mental_health_and_behaviour_in_schools__.pdf

just the MHFA and sometimes also with a head of year, tracking young people who have been referred, and discussing strategies for support.

The DMHL must ensure these key members of the pastoral team are properly trained in how to approach the young person, how to conduct non-judgemental listening, spotting the signs of various mental health challenges and encouraging the young person where to access help and support in the school and in the community. The school will feel the positive impact of this type of training and CPD investment. I would strongly suggest a one-day inset for these staff (see Appendix 1 for more on this).

The Youth Mental Health First Aider course[2] also offers excellent training that has been designed and proven to equip educators with the right skills to help young people and how to approach those difficult conversations or situations.

It is important at this point to remind staff that it is not their place to diagnose, but if there is a concern, it is advisable that a report is filed and a triage is carried out of the young person to see if their primary need is a learning need, a pastoral need or a mental health need. There are a number of identification and measurement tools, such as the Strengths and Difficulties Questionnaire (SDQ) and Boxall Profile, which can support this process.[3]

What is the Strengths and Difficulties Questionnaire?

The Strengths and Difficulties Questionnaire (SDQ) is a brief emotional and behavioural screening questionnaire for children and young people and can be accessed via its own website,[4,5] or via the Heads Together Mental Healthy Schools' website in their Resource Library section.[6]

What is the Boxall Profile?

The Boxall Profile is an online assessment tool for children and young people's social, emotional and behavioural development, and can help with early identification and assessment, setting individualized, achievable targets that reinforce target behaviour and skills and track progress, and it can be accessed via the Boxall Profile website.[7]

---

2   See https://mhfaengland.org/individuals/youth
3   Department for Education (2018) *Mental Health and Behaviour in Schools*. London: HMSO. Available at: https://assets.publishing.service.gov.uk/government/uploads/system/uploads/attachment_data/file/755135/Mental_health_and_behaviour_in_schools__.pdf
4   www.sdqinfo.org
5   www.mentallyhealthyschools.org.uk/resources/the-strengths-and-difficulties-questionnaire-sdq
6   www.mentallyhealthyschools.org.uk/resources
7   https://boxallprofile.org/#more

This initial assessment is important because it will help the school consider the best support plan that can be actioned to secure impact. Once the triage is complete, and if it is clear that the young person needs support with their mental health challenge, it is important that the DMHL works closely with the pastoral team so that:

- The student can be supported appropriately in class at breaks and lunchtimes and, if necessary, be supported with peer relationships.

- The student can be supported by their tutor, which helps build a strong relationship with a trusted adult.

- Reasonable adjustments are made to the school's policies, the physical environment, the support it offers, and how it responds in situations to that individual.

- Parents and guardians are involved, and the dialogue is had with them.

- The student knows where to go for further information or support should they want to talk about their own, their peers' or their family's mental health or wellbeing.

- An intervention, agreed by the students and/or parents and pastoral leader, is put into place, and is then closely tracked and reviewed.

If the young person is given anything from a one-off one-to-one, group intervention or six-week intervention programme it is vital that the relevant pastoral team members working directly with the student are fully informed and liaise directly with the DMHL. Once the intervention is complete, it is important that the DMHL completes an assessment to see if the agreed outcomes were met (see Appendix 3), and whether another intervention should be put in place and/or a referral to an external agency.

5

Working with Parents

Adopting a whole-school approach to mental wellbeing means the mantras *we all have mental health* and *mental health is everybody's business* need to be shared regularly. It is widely regarded that parents and schools are a 50/50 partnership in bringing up and educating children, and that if both parties work together, then there is consistency for the child, and the life skills we are teaching are more likely to be legitimized. These mantras should therefore be shared with parents, and parents should be included in the conversation about supporting the mental health and wellbeing of their child.

It is vital that schools focus on a range of different approaches to work productively with parents, ensuring clear communication and a positive dialogue around mental health and safeguarding issues.

The DMHL should have a three-tiered approach to working with parents:

Tier 1

Ensure all parents and carers are aware of what mental health is and what level of support is available to all students in the school. The DMHL can ensure there is clear online information about mental health and what the warning signs are, with hyperlinks to where they can get additional support in the community if they are concerned about their child. It is also advisable to have a section that deals with stress and exams and how parents can support at home. In the weekly planner you will see I talk about building the school website to ensure parents are aware of the lunchtime support and self-referral opportunities for students if they need to talk. It is important that parents know what is available, but also what is not available. For example, at our school, we don't offer counselling services. In one school where I worked, we managed to host workshops on *resilient parenting* and how to bring up resilient teenagers. In another school we built our own bespoke mental health and wellbeing app that they could download, 'BHCS My World', with sections on My Mind, My Body and My Relationships offering advice and where to get support. We have embraced the power of audio and created podcasts for teenagers and parents on FAQ about mental health and teenagers, including exam stress and dealing with anxiety.

Tier 2

When students have made a disclosure or have been referred by a staff member, a triage has been completed and if it is clear the student is facing mild to moderate mental health challenges, a Tier 2 intervention will kick in. Parents and carers will be invited in, with their child, to openly discuss the difficulties the child is having in the school environment, and at home, too, and how best the school can support the child to ensure they keep coming in to school to receive their education. This might involve making reasonable adjustments to the child's timetable, how they are supported in lessons and at lunchtimes, and any additional group or one-to-one sessions with MHFAs of empathetic listening and signposting to internal and external resources, which will help unpick their concerns and think about strategies for coping. To measure impact regarding the interventions, a set of outcomes will be agreed at the start with the parents, in terms of mental, emotional and behavioural responses, and these will be reviewed again at the end. The child may only need a one-off individual mental health care plan or their case may need to be reviewed again and another programme put in place; either way, it is vital that the parents are invited in at all stages.

Another way that the school can have more targeted parental involvement is by forming a parent focus group. One school started #parentwellbeingambassadors to ensure that there was constant feedback from the parents on how they could create a school community that was values-led and able to build a culture of wellbeing.

Tier 3

If a student's mental health need is more than mild to moderate and they require a formal referral and the intervention of external agencies and their specialist therapeutic interventions, the role of the DMHL and the school team will effectively step back as the external agency will probably deal directly with the parents and the student. They may still meet on the school premises, but unless the parents give their consent for the information to be shared with the school, all information will be shared directly with the parents. This is discussed in more detail in the brief on working with mental health teams (see Chapter 7).

6

Inputting Data and Tracking Outcomes

It is essential that records are up to date, accurate and rigorous, with as much detail given as possible. Ofsted inspectors will want to see excellent child protection and safeguarding policies, and this will include the mental health and wellbeing policy or guidance document and how the school has responded to disclosures and referrals. Child safety is always the priority, and this will involve looking at the school's register, safeguarding policies and child protection files. Note: If you fail child protection, you are automatically placed into 'inadequate' measures. If a child is not safe, the school is deemed 'not fit for purpose'.

As the DSL is under pressure to ensure files, policies and interventions are up to date, it is the DMHL's responsibility to ensure that all data and information regarding students facing mental health challenges are also kept up to date, with ease of access for the DMHL to share and talk about.

It is the DMHL's duty to keep a record of all meetings, to share the minutes and to ensure that all interventions, from one-off conversations about a student to longer interventions, are recorded, tracked and impact is measured. When the DMHL makes a referral to the mental health support team, an additional triage will be completed based on what the school knows, and some further forensic 'drilling down' will take place to really understand the case and the needs of the young person. Up-to-date and accurate record keeping will help enormously here as they build a profile of a student.

Most schools use CPOMS (a software solution for monitoring safeguarding, wellbeing and all pastoral issues) to raise a safeguarding concern. Some schools, in addition, use provision mapping (ProvisionMap has features designed to help manage SEND (students with special educational needs and disabilities) and Pupil Premium (disadvantaged students who qualify for additional school funding by the government to improve their attainment)) to help track interventions and outcomes; others use simple spreadsheets and track interventions that way. Either way, it is important that the weekly referrals and interventions are tracked, recorded, outcomes measured and the school is able to make an informed decision when referring to external agencies or mental health support teams.

I would have a weekly meeting with the MHFA to track interventions and referrals and how best we could support students, staff and families as well as tracking interventions with an external agency.

7

Working with the Mental Health Support Teams and External Agencies

Schools should be aware of the role they are expected to play in any multi-agency safeguarding arrangements when it comes to supporting the mental health and safeguarding of a child. Full details regarding early help and the role of schools can be found in Part 1 of *Keeping Children Safe in Education*[1] and Chapter 1 of *Working Together to Safeguard Children*.[2]

The DMHL should be in regular contact with their local health and wellbeing boards and health services, and the school should have access to local educational psychology services and a range of effective, evidence-based services in place for support on mental health, including specialist children and young people's mental health services (CYPMHS).

For many schools, interagency work will be around working with the following services or groups:

- The School Nursing Service: Support from this service could come from presentations in assemblies to seeing the students directly. The nurses will sometimes offer several sessions with the students because often behind a 'medical' reason for low attendance, for example, there is also a mental health concern. The service can work with mental health and wellbeing teams in schools to identify vulnerable children, and it is also able to provide advice on local projects and refer to other services offering coordinated support. The service offers family support and can direct the school to local mental health organizations to help the child and their family better understand the challenges facing the young person.

- YPI (Young Person's Information) or YC (Young Counselling) groups: These are often free mental health mentoring services led by qualified youth

1   Department for Education (2020) *Keeping Children Safe in Education: Statutory Guidance for Schools and Colleges*. London: HMSO. Available at: https://assets.publishing.service.gov.uk/government/uploads/system/uploads/attachment_data/file/912592/Keeping_children_safe_in_education_Sep_2020.pdf

2   Department for Education (2015) *Working Together to Safeguard Children: Statutory Guidance on Inter-Agency Working to Safeguard and Promote the Welfare of Children*. [Updated in 2020.] Available at: www.gov.uk/government/publications/working-together-to-safeguard-children--2

mental health mentors or counsellors. This service is good because it sees a wide range of students in an informal setting, and because it is run by young adults themselves; students can sometimes relate to them more.

- Family Support Service: Most councils will also have this service, which offers a range of workshops from anxiety to domestic abuse support. People working for this service are also qualified and trained to work with students who have had adverse childhood experiences (ACEs). The service is often funded by a local council, which means it is free and facilitated by non-school staff.

Ultimately, all schools would like on their wish list having a trained counsellor in school, for a few days each week, or at least more key workers who could support students and staff working with them. Schools need more adults helping with interventions if they are truly going to be pre-emptive and proactive.

Whilst I was writing this book, the UK government's much talked about mental health support teams, documented in the Green Paper,[3] were actively working in a select few trailblazer counties. The idea is that new mental health support teams are supervised by NHS children and young people's mental health staff and linked to groups of schools and colleges. The mental health support teams will work with the DSLs for mental health in schools and colleges, and provide support for addressing the needs of children with mild to moderate mental health issues. They will also provide a link with more specialist NHS mental health services so that children can more swiftly access help they need.

I spoke to Jamie Douglas, the operations manager for mental health support teams in Oxford City and North Oxfordshire, about working with the DMHL in schools and what the relationship can and should look like working with the mental health support teams.

The mental health support teams are generally made up of about four educational mental health practitioners (EMHPs)[4] with a clinical lead. The clinical lead looks after supervision for the EMHPs and allocates the teams. This team is responsible for anything up to 8000 students. Their remit is to support children and young people who have mild to moderate mental health needs – essentially, those who don't (yet) meet the CAMHS threshold for referral.

---

3   Department of Health and Department for Education (2017) *Transforming Children and Young People's Mental Health Provision: A Green Paper.* Cm 9523. London: HMSO, p.21. Available at: https://assets. publishing.service.gov.uk/government/uploads/system/uploads/attachment_data/file/664855/ Transforming_children_and_young_people_s_mental_health_provision.pdf

4   www.reading.ac.uk/module/document.aspx?modP=PYMPES&modYR=1819

According to NICE guidelines:[5]

A *mild mental health problem* is when a person has a small number of symptoms that have a limited effect on their daily life. A *moderate mental health problem* is when a person has more symptoms that can make their daily life much more difficult than usual. A *severe mental health problem* is when a person has many symptoms that can make their daily life extremely difficult.

It is vital that the DMHL and mental health and wellbeing team in the school set up a good working relationship with the mental health support teams if they want to see long-term change and a culture that is proactive and pre-emptive as opposed to reactive. There are a few things the DMHL can do to ensure the working relationship is successful and has a positive impact on children:

- Give up time, every six weeks, to meet the mental health support teams. Don't cancel. This is important for continuity and ensuring discussions can be had about the whole-school culture and individual cases.

- Provide them with a reliable and suitable person who will be their weekly contact when visiting the school, preferably someone who is not always teaching. In this instance it could be the MHFA. In smaller schools it might be the head teacher who is also the DSL. In addition, provide them with a suitable venue in which to meet the pupils or parents.

- Recognize that the degree of support will vary from school to school depending on the audit completed of the mental health needs and provisions already existing in the school. For some schools that are in some way embedding a culture of mental health and wellbeing, these mental health support teams will be another route for interventions. For schools that have made hardly any progress, these mental health support teams could be the school's main and only provider in tackling mental health needs in the school.

- Keep and provide records and information so that they can build an accurate picture.

- Get consent from the parents to make the referral.

---

5   NICE (National Institute for Health and Care Excellence) (2011) *Common Mental Health Problems: Identification and Pathways to Care*. Clinical Guideline 123. London: NICE. Available at: www.nice.org.uk/guidance/cg123/ifp/chapter/Common-mental-health-problems

- Refer using the online web-based referral form and then file the referral form for the school's own data tracking of interventions being given to young people.

- Be aware that once the referral is made a triage will be completed based on what the school knows, doing some forensic 'drilling down' to really understand the case and the needs of the young person.

If the case is referred to a specialist agency because it is deemed as a 'severe' level of mental health need, the EMHP will contact the parents and most of the six-week intervention will be had with the parents from here on, as the focus will be parent-led. The intervention could be, but not necessarily, a cognitive behavioural therapy (CBT). If the child is over 12, then a direct one-to-one meeting will also be had with the child without the parent necessarily being there.

Finally, information about the outcomes of the intervention will only be shared with the school if the parent consents.

8

Suggested Training for the Designated Mental Health Leads

There are several training options for DMHLs. To get you started, here are some great organisations, who I all know personally and can confidently endorse. They are very experienced mental health experts & trainers who are doing fantastic work in training the DMHL with online or live training or for the DMHL to contact and bring into their schools to deliver high impact quality training.

Creative Education

If you visit Dr Pooky Knightsmith's Creative Education platform,[1] there are over 200 bite-size on-demand courses you can do, from a whole-school mental health and wellbeing approach to guidance for interventions for supporting young people. Also offered are live webinars and bespoke training.

Changing States of Mind

Lucinda Powell offers training and consultancy that applies psychological principles to the school setting to improve whole school mental health and wellbeing. She works with schools and DMHLs to help embed a whole school approach. She can also provide a wide variety of Mental Health training for staff including on exam anxiety, positive classroom wellbeing, teenage brain development, studying to reduce stress as well as bespoke workshops. You can hear more on her podcast 'Psychology in the Classroom' (available on Apple Podcasts, Spotify and Amazon).

Growing Great Schools

Growing Great Schools was established by Sue Roffey with partners around the world to promote ways for all schools to become great schools. They provide training, globally, on many aspects of behaviour, school and student wellbeing, school leadership and social and emotional learning, as well as consultancy on all aspects of student and school wellbeing.

---

1   https://elearning.creativeeducation.co.uk/available-courses

Innovating Minds

If you sign up to Innovating Minds, you can access designated mental health leads training, use the EduPod platform and access clinical support. The platform enables you to audit, evaluate and plan your mental health strategy. There is also a series of free webinars and resources endorsed by mental health clinicians where you can upskill your practice as a DMHL.

Kelley Hanaghan

Kelly is a consultant with The Education People who has worked systemically with some of the most challenging communities by supporting families, with the strategies to thrive from adversities. The Current training being offered is:

- Training for a whole school approach for Designated Mental Health Leads

- Senior Mental Health Lead training

- Staff Wellbeing Training for Wellbeing Leads in Education.

Teachappy Training with Adrian Bethune

Teachappy offers training and workshops for teaching staff on using positive psychology to develop the happiness and wellbeing of children and staff. Delivered live in school or remotely, plus they now have online, learn at your own pace course too.

Worth-it

Worth-it offers training grounded in the mental wellbeing sciences of positive psychology and coaching psychology and can be contacted for training for schools to promote wellbeing and resilience outcomes for children and young people and coaching for school staff.

Carnegie Centre of Excellence for Mental Health in Schools

The first university to have a PGDip and Master's Programme in Leadership of Mental Health and Wellbeing in Schools. The current two courses are as follows:

Development Programme for School Mental Health Lead

The programme explores what effective whole-school mental health policy looks like, and the steps needed to ensure effective implementation and review. It covers applying key mental health Department for Education (England) policies within school, understanding the role of the DSL for mental health, evaluating current practice and using this to create a highly targeted mental health development plan.

On completion of the programme, you will have grown your capacity and confidence for leading whole-school mental health strategies. You will also have developed a deeper understanding of the latest thinking on effective mental health practice and improved your ability to identify children at risk of poor mental health and implement effective supportive strategies. You will be able to identify and implement improvement strategies and form a professional network of peers who are leading mental health in their schools.

The programme is split into three units:

- Unit 1: The whole-school approach to mental health – strategy and practice.

- Unit 2: Working effectively – the DSL for mental health, governance and key colleagues.

- Unit 3: Leading and embedding change that improves mental health.

This programme is for senior mental health leads responsible for mental health policy and strategy across the whole school.

Those who wish to take their learning further have gone on to study a PGDip or Master's on the Leadership of School Mental Health and Wellbeing, as below:

Postgraduate Diploma or Master's in Leadership of School Mental Health and Wellbeing (Distance Learning)

Working alongside fellow school leaders and teachers, you will gain an understanding of the evidence of effective whole-school mental health, and be able to apply this to your role as a school leader. You will learn how to recognize issues such as low self-esteem, anxiety and depression, so that you can take early steps to improve the mental health of the children in your care, developing sophisticated and original interventions to build their resilience and nurture appropriate coping mechanisms.

Finally, you can always get in touch with me via LinkedIn (Clare Erasmus), where I can either try to help you myself or put you in touch with these experts in the field delivering accessible and relevant training and offering practical advice and tips on how you can ensure your school is preemptive and proactive in supporting mild to moderate mental health challenges, working with the mental health support teams as well as training and upskilling the DMHL.

9

Designated Mental Health Lead Self-Care and Wellbeing

The pressure to role model good wellbeing and not appear exhausted yourself is a tough one in an educational setting. I completely recognize that to begin with this role will be absorbed along with other middle management and senior leadership roles, and so feeling overburdened is quite possible. That is why in this planner, in every week, I encourage you, as the DMHL, to practise self-care. There is a weekly reminder to include self-care in your daily routine and a section to practise gratitude and record your mental wellbeing action for the week.

Also, at the back of the book is an alphabetical wellbeing guide for things the DMHL can practise in both a school and a home setting (see Appendix 2).

In addition to 'walking the talk', the role of the DMHL can feel very isolated, and so I urge readers to connect with other DMHLs. Twitter, Opogo[1] and LinkedIn can be extremely helpful as they all host a community of mental health leads who regularly blog and share best practice. The moment I realized I was leading on mental wellbeing I immediately connected with wellbeing warriors using social media platforms, which also helped me connect with DMHLs in my local borough and council. My handle is @cerasmusteach on Twitter, Opogo and LinkedIn, and if you connect with me and tell me you want to connect with others, I'm very happy to link you in with people who inspire me and organizations that have structures to support our role in a school (but please reference my book so I know where the floods of requests are coming from!).

---

[1]   https://opogo.com/teachers

Section 2

PLANNER

10

An Introduction to the Year Planner

A school that aims to adopt a culture of mental health and wellbeing will need a whole-school approach. There are many key stakeholders who all need to be involved and working with each other. It is important to write a yearly planner that feeds into the school development plan (SDP).

The different strands for a whole-school approach are about having focus on:

1. Leadership, strategy and governance. This thread will focus on governance, student and staff consultation, the curriculum and wider curriculum, ensuring it all feeds into the strategic vision.

2. Staff professional development for mental health and wellbeing and guidance for staff in supporting their own mental health. This is all about training and ensuring there are dedicated inset days or CPD ensuring staff are trained on children's mental health and that mental health is everybody's business, not just the DMHL's and MHFA's. Plus, it's about ensuring staff mental health and wellbeing is high on the agenda when it comes to the leadership team seeking to prioritize workload reduction, destigmatizing the conversation about mental health and ensuring the school actively promotes a culture of wellbeing, kindness, care and trust.

3. Student mental wellbeing and identifying students at risk. This is all about doing an audit of what the school is already doing for students, listening to the students' voices, ensuring what is put in place is commensurate with students' needs and ensuring the safeguarding of all students with early and relevant interventions.

4. Curriculum planning and resources. This is all about ensuring your school is meeting the government's new statutory PSHE requirements regarding health education, relationships education and mental health. Teaching about mental health and emotional wellbeing could be delivered through the PSHE curriculum and threaded through the wider curriculum that the school aims to offer. The DMHL needs to have an overview of this and ensure the focus is to make sure that pupils can make an informed choice about their own and their peers' mental health and wellbeing, and that they

are aware of support both in the school and the community, and what are negative and positive coping strategies.

5. Working with parents and the wider community. It is widely regarded that parents and schools are a 50/50 partnership in bringing up and educating children, and that if both parties work together, then there is consistency for the child and the life skills we are teaching are more likely to be accepted. The success of any school mental wellbeing programme is also dependent on the role of the parents in engaging in mental wellbeing conversations, interventions and promoting lifestyle choices that encourage positive mental wellbeing. This thread is about ensuring that the parents are involved and are encouraged to actively contribute to the culture of care and wellbeing.

6. Working with external agencies and provision of support services. This thread means that each term the DMHL ensures that referral pathways to external agencies are clearly understood and all working parties are debriefed and given accurate records.

7. Assessing, tracking and recording concerns and interventions. This thread is all about due diligence and ensuring that all parties are clear about the referral pathways for a safeguarding concern, that cases are accurately triaged and relevant interventions are put into place and then clearly tracked and assessed against clear outcomes.

Once you have written your yearly planner, these threads will then feed into your termly planners. You will see I have put together a list of suggestions for each term that the DMHL could consider. Obviously, each school's demographic is different, as are their needs, and the approach will differ slightly for primary and secondary schools. What I have tried to ensure is that each thread is revisited each term, and the DMHL can track progress, from setting up structures, quality assuring policies, introducing concepts and then embedding the culture of mental health and wellbeing in all areas of school practice over the course of a school year. Finally, the DMHL will be able to track the progress each term, ticking the relevant boxes: Some evidence of being embedded or fully embedded and evidenced.

11

Year Planner

Whole-school mental health and wellbeing approach	Specific focus	Some evidence of being embedded	Fully embedded and evidenced
1. Leadership, strategy and governance	• To work closely with the governing body, the wellbeing governor and the head teacher on the strategic vision.		
	• To ensure that mental health and wellbeing support structures relating to supporting staff and students are placed on the SDP, including training, and these are also evidenced and integrated into policies and guidance documents led by the DMHL.		
	• The school actively promotes a culture of mental wellbeing in the curriculum, extra curriculum and wider community.		
	• The school commits to a whole-school approach, either through a mental health award or Kitemark scheme.		
2. Staff professional development for mental health and wellbeing: guidance for staff in supporting their own mental health	• To ensure all staff feel supported and that the school has a 'health-promoting' working environment where kindness, care and trust are cornerstones for all working relationships.		
	• To ensure the school management is constantly reviewing teacher workload, which links to mental health, and workload expectations are realistic and achievable, building a work ethic so that there is school–home balance.		
	• Building a culture where all staff feel valued.		
	• There are clear support procedures if a staff member feels the need to share concerns about their mental health.		
	• All staff are all trained to spot the signs and listen without judgement and to understand that mental health is everyone's responsibility.		
	• School staff cannot act as mental health experts and should not try to diagnose conditions. However, they should ensure they have clear systems and processes in place for identifying possible mental health challenges, including clear referral and accountability processes.		
	• Staff self-care is modelled from the leadership team and actively encouraged.		
	• There is a culture of offering supervision for teachers and educators whose role involves supporting children and young people with issues affecting their wellbeing and mental health such as stress or anxiety.		

Student mental wellbeing and identifying students at risk	• Safeguarding is effective.
	• Coordinate interventions for students who are identified as being of concern, and ensure these interventions are measured against measurable outcomes.
	• Ensure there are robust working links with children and young people's mental health services so that the school can refer when appropriate.
	• Students are listened to and feel safe.
	• The student voice is active, for example, through wellbeing ambassadors, anti-bullying ambassadors and Freedom 2B ambassadors.
	• Structures and spaces are set up so that students can self-refer, for example, into the wellbeing zone or #wellbeingsquare where there are trained adults and ambassadors.
	• All students receive age-appropriate lessons on the topic of what mental health is, what steps they can take to support positive mental health, and what the signs of a mental health challenge are.
	• All students are signposted to relevant helplines and procedures, either on the website or through a bespoke mental wellbeing app.
	• Students are encouraged to have another route for interventions found in the school extra curriculum encouraging all students to feel part of the wider school community.
	• Student mental health and wellbeing is seen as being as important as academic excellence, and the one should not be achieved at the expense of the other.
	• Student character strengths are recognized as well as resilience, and these are praised alongside academic excellence and effort.
4. Curriculum planning and resources	• Students can explain accurately and confidently how to keep themselves healthy.
	• Students have an emotional literacy about their own mental wellbeing, and they make informed choices about healthy eating, fitness and their emotional and mental wellbeing.
	• Students have an age-appropriate understanding of healthy relationships, and are confident in staying safe from abuse and exploitation.
	• Students have an excellent understanding of how to stay safe online and of the dangers of inappropriate use of mobile technology and social networking sites.

Whole-school mental health and wellbeing approach	Specific focus	Some evidence of being embedded	Fully embedded and evidenced
5. Working with parents and the wider community	• Parents are involved in interventions that support their children's mental health and wellbeing, and are part of the early identification of mental health challenges.		
	• Parents have access to information about mental health that provides guidance and opportunities for support in the school and in the local community.		
	• Parents feel involved in being part of building a culture of mental wellbeing, and are regularly invited to share their views.		
6. Working with external agencies and provision of support services	• The DMHL and staff work effectively with external partners to support students who are at risk or who are the subject of a multi-agency plan.		
	• Referral pathways to external agencies are clearly understood.		
	• The mental health support teams (cited in the Green Paper) are debriefed and records are kept up to date to ensure external agencies have all the relevant information available.		
	• The DMHL and staff make themselves available to accommodate and work alongside external agencies.		
	• The school is part of a borough or community mental health transformation plan that seeks to share best practice and resources.		
7. Assessing, tracking and recording concerns and interventions	• The DMHL has a clear plan on how safeguarding concerns are raised; how an effective triage will take place; all those in school receiving interventions are clearly tracked; and outcomes and objectives are recorded on an individual student support mental wellbeing plan.		

Chapter 12

Term Plans

Autumn Term 1a	Strategic focus	Some evidence of being embedded	Fully embedded and evidenced
1. Leadership, strategy and governance	• Meet with the DSL and plan mental health early morning briefings interspersed with SEND briefings.		
	• Set performance management targets in line with the DMHL role.		
	• Write or review the mental health and wellbeing guidance documents or policies for staff and students and submit to the SLT and governors for ratification.		
	• Work with the school governor overseeing mental wellbeing.		
	• Read the criteria for the mental health award or Kitemark scheme your school has committed to and conduct an audit of current provisions. (If you have not signed up to a mental health award for your school, I strongly suggest you do so as it will give you a mandate to bring about change).		
2. Staff professional development for mental health and wellbeing	• Awareness raising amongst staff and students of your role and who the MHFA and wellbeing ambassadors are. Deliver either in an inset slot, podcast, video or email.		
	• When photos are taken of the DSL and safeguarding team and put up around the school, make sure they are also taken of the DMHL and MHFA, and have the mental health and wellbeing team visible in strategic places.		
	• Invite staff to join the Staff Wellbeing Action Group (SWAGS, a platform for staff voice) and arrange your first meeting (make sure minutes are always shared with the SLT).		
	• Arrange with the SLT for a staff wellbeing room to be allocated and set up, a place for mindfulness and quiet.		
	• Pre-plan a series of 10-minute early morning mental health briefings (see Appendix 1) that will take place during the year to update or raise awareness amongst colleagues. These can also be presented by other members of the pastoral support team.		
	• Plan an inset slot once a year where you deliver training based on the needs of the school (see Appendix 1).		
3. Student mental wellbeing and identifying students at risk	• Train the mental health and wellbeing ambassadors.		
	• Check and set up a staff rota for the wellbeing zone (where students meet every lunchtime to self-refer). Open the wellbeing zone.		
	• Plan World Mental Health Day for 10 October.		
	• Meet the mental health ambassadors weekly to ensure their safeguarding and to discuss events, presentations and activities being run in the wellbeing zone.		
	• Identify and review the list of students at risk and oversee strategies for support and interventions, establishing links with external agencies and professionals. Ensure the individual student support mental wellbeing plan is written.		

4. Curriculum planning and resources	- 10 September is World Suicide Prevention Day, so arrange mental health curriculum lessons, assemblies or awareness posters about where support is available. - Review the mental health curriculum roll-out for Autumn Term 1a. - Plan World Mental Health Day for 10 October and arrange mental health curriculum lessons, assemblies or awareness posters about it.
5. Working with parents and the wider community	- Develop a website giving parents clear information about the mental health support in your school or where to get support outside in the community. This could be written, as podcasts or short films. Aim to engage. - Review information about where to get mental health support on the school website and check it is up to date. - Meet parents whose children have been identified as needing additional support and early interventions and involve them in the process.
6. Working with external agencies and provision of support services	- Connect with a local consortium to discuss the wellbeing protocol in the region and working with the mental health support teams (cited in the Green Paper) in schools. - Connect with local external services such as young carers, mental health nurses, Rotary Youth Services, etc.
7. Assessing, tracking and recording safeguarding concerns and interventions	- Each week have a line management meeting with the MHFA to discuss safeguarding issues, students at risk and strategies for support, overseeing interventions and establishing links with external agencies and professionals. Ensure the individual student support mental wellbeing plan is filled in and parents are contacted.
Additional points I want to add that are specific to my school	

Autumn Term 1b	Strategic focus	Some evidence of being embedded	Fully embedded and evidenced
1. Leadership, strategy and governance	• Ensure staff wellbeing and student mental wellbeing guidance documents or policies have been ratified by governors and are available on the school website with other policies.		
	• Once the self-audit has been completed for the mental health award or Kitemark your school is going for, roll out relevant surveys to identify strengths and weaknesses and which areas need to be developed.		
	• Investigate the idea of having a therapy dog with research, training and a policy. Do the groundwork.		
	• Meet with the DSL and review safeguarding and mental health and the process from making a referral to triage to follow-up to measuring impact. Identify young people of concern and interventions being put in place.		
2. Staff professional development for mental health and wellbeing	• Request and deliver an inset day slot where you train staff on signs to look out for or setting up safe classrooms teaching a mental health lesson as part of PSHE delivery or how to practise and teach basic mindfulness for students, as in grounded breathing.		
	• Continue mental health early morning briefings (see Appendix 1).		
	• Meet the Staff Wellbeing Action Group (SWAGS).		
	• Have the official opening of the staff wellbeing room. Encourage mindfulness activities to happen here before school, lunchtime and after school.		
3. Student mental wellbeing and identifying students at risk	• Meet the mental health ambassadors weekly to ensure their safeguarding; discuss events, presentations and activities being run in the #wellbeingsquare or wellbeing zone.		
	• Roll out the student wellbeing survey.		
	• Identify and review the list of students at risk and oversee strategies for support and interventions, establishing links with external agencies and professionals. Ensure the individual student support mental wellbeing plan is filled in and parents are contacted.		
4. Curriculum planning and resources	• The Anti-Bullying Week is in November, so ensure assemblies are delivered by the students and relevant videos and case studies shared on links with mental health. Focus on where support is and strategies for dealing with bullying or a breakdown in friendships.		
	• Review the mental health curriculum roll-out for Autumn Term 1b, focusing on mental health lessons.		

5. Working with parents and the wider community	• Plan #familyMH5aday (see Appendix 6) roll-out for the last weeks of term as part of the Christmas theme for focusing on #GREATvalues (see Appendix 6). • Send out articles in the student and parent newsletter advertising it.		
6. Working with external agencies and provision of support services	• Arrange to meet the local young carers support group, CAMHS working parties, school nurses for your school area, etc.		
7. Assessing, tracking and recording safeguarding concerns and interventions	• Each week have a line management meeting with the MHFA to discuss safeguarding issues, students at risk and strategies for support, overseeing interventions and establishing links with external agencies and professionals. • Ensure all safeguarding concerns are logged, followed up on and interventions are tracked. • Review cases referred and make a list of the recurring mental health challenges in your school or community, and plan awareness workshops and inset days for all staff, e.g. self-harm; suicide ideation; exam anxiety and revision stress; eating disorders.		
Additional points I want to add that are specific to my school			

Spring Term 2a	Strategic focus	Some evidence of being embedded	Fully embedded and evidenced
1. Leadership, strategy and governance	• Roll out 'You said, We did' in response to staff and student mental wellbeing surveys. Go for marginal gains and quick wins.		
	• Plan long-term interventions based on the survey results and build an action plan into these termly plans. Always keep referring to the Kitemark or mental health award criteria your school is going for.		
	• Review progress of the mental health award. How many of the criteria have you met so far?		
	• Meet with the DSL and review safeguarding and mental health and the process from making a referral to triage to follow-up to measuring impact. Identify the young person of concern and the interventions being put in place.		
2. Staff professional development for mental health and wellbeing	• Train staff in mental health briefing on eating disorders: the signs, the types, how to respond, support in school and help in the local community (see Appendix 1).		
	• Meet the Staff Wellbeing Action Group (SWAGS). Feed back the results of the survey and agree strategies moving forward to support staff mental health (ensure all minutes are shared with the SLT and governors).		
	• Coordinate and plan a staff mental wellbeing Time to Talk Day[1] that happens in early February and that brings the nation together to get talking and break the silence around mental health problems.		
	• Advertise in the staff room. Host a Tea and Talk session.		
3. Student mental wellbeing and identifying students at risk	• Meet the mental health ambassadors weekly, ensuring their safeguarding.		
	• Create a Year 11 exam revision timetable that includes learning to take time out and focus on the #GREATvalues (Give, Relate, Exercise, Awareness, Try something new). Make sure it is written into their revision timetable. This teaches young people strategies for coping with stress.		
	• Identify and review the list of students at risk and oversee strategies for support and interventions, establishing links with external agencies and professionals. Ensure the individual student support mental wellbeing plan is filled in and parents are contacted.		

---

1 www.time-to-change.org.uk/get-involved/time-talk-day

4. Curriculum planning and resources	• Review the mental health curriculum roll-out for Spring Term 1a roll-out. • Wellbeing Valentine's Day. Talk about self-compassion and learning to love yourself. • Plan for Eating Disorders Week with the mental health ambassadors. • Eating Disorders Awareness Week (EDAW) 2021 takes place from early March.[2]		
5. Working with parents and the wider community	• Update the website on National Awareness days. Send out articles in the newsletter; record podcasts on eating disorders and Time to Talk to destigmatize.		
6. Working with external agencies and provision of support services	• Set up links with charities for eating disorders and ask for workshops or presentations to be made available for students.		
7. Assessing, tracking and recording safeguarding concerns and interventions	• Each week have a line management meeting with the MHFA and/or pastoral team to discuss safeguarding issues, students at risk and strategies for support, overseeing interventions and establishing links with external agencies and professionals. Ensure the individual student support mental wellbeing plan is filled in and parents are contacted.		
Additional points I want to add that are specific to my school			

Spring Term 2b	Strategic focus	Some evidence of being embedded	Fully embedded and evidenced
1. Leadership, strategy and governance	• Continue mental health early morning briefings.		
	• Review progress of mental health award or Kitemark status. How many of the criteria have you met so far?		
	• Meet with the DSL and review safeguarding and mental health and the process from making a referral to triage to follow-up to measuring impact. Identify the young person of concern and interventions being put in place.		
2. Staff professional development for mental health and wellbeing	• Meet the Staff Wellbeing Action Group (SWAGS).		
	• Train staff in the mental health briefing on stress awareness for both staff and student wellbeing (see Appendix 1).		
	• Plan for Stress Awareness Month – April marks its start![3]		
3. Student mental wellbeing and identifying students at risk	• Meet the mental health ambassadors weekly, safeguarding their mental health.		
	• Plan for Children's Mental Health Week,[4] which takes place in February.		
	• World Bipolar Day[5] takes place every year on 30 March. Bipolar disorder is a serious mental illness that affects over a million people in the UK alone.		
	• Identify and review the list of students at risk and oversee strategies for support and interventions, establishing links with external agencies and professionals. Ensure the individual student support mental wellbeing plan is written.		
4. Curriculum planning and resources	• Review the mental health curriculum for Spring Term 2b.		

3   www.stress.org.uk/national-stress-awareness-month-2019
4   www.awarenessdays.com/awareness-days-calendar/childrens-mental-health-week-2020
5   www.isbd.org/world-bipolar-day

5. Working with parents and the wider community	• Update the website on National Awareness days. • Send out articles in the newsletter. • Share podcasts from well-known celebrities/record your own or share media which will help develop greater awareness	
6. Working with external agencies and provision of support services	• Review your assessment and tracking sheet of students working with external agencies and support services. Check that progress on interventions has been updated and contact numbers and names are up to date. • Check what free training is available for your support and pastoral staff from local county services.	
7. Assessing, tracking and recording safeguarding concerns and interventions	• Each week have a line management meeting with the MHFA and/or pastoral team to discuss safeguarding issues, students at risk and strategies for support, overseeing interventions and establishing links with external agencies and professionals. Ensure the individual student support mental wellbeing plan is filled in and parents are contacted.	
Additional points I want to add that are specific to my school		

Summer Term 3a	Strategic focus	Some evidence of being embedded	Fully embedded and evidenced
1. Leadership, strategy and governance	• Continue mental health early morning briefings.		
	• Review progress of mental health award or Kitemark status. How many of the criteria have you met so far?		
	• Meet with the DSL and review safeguarding and mental health and the process from making a referral to triage to follow-up to measuring impact. Identify the young person of concern and interventions being put in place.		
2. Staff professional development for mental health and wellbeing	• Meet the Staff Wellbeing Action Group (SWAGS). Review strategies put in place since the survey. Feed back minutes to the SLT.		
	• Train staff in mental health briefing on bipolar disorder, body image and awareness of mental health illnesses.		
3. Student mental wellbeing and identifying students at risk	• Meet the mental health ambassadors weekly, and supervise their safeguarding.		
	• Identify and review the list of students at risk and oversee strategies for support and interventions, establishing links with external agencies and professionals. Ensure the individual student support mental wellbeing plan is written.		
4. Curriculum planning and resources	• Review the mental health curriculum for Summer Term 1a.		
	• Plan lessons to coincide with Mental Health Awareness Week.[6] Hosted by the Mental Health Foundation, this will take place from mid-May.		
	• Each year has a different theme – build a campaign around this year's theme.		
5. Working with parents and the wider community	• Update the website on National Awareness days. Send out articles in the newsletter; share podcasts and media to raise awareness or create your own.		

6   www.mentalhealth.org.uk/campaigns/mental-health-awareness-week

6. Working with external agencies and provision of support services	• Book in speakers for assemblies and inset days for the next year. • Review and update your register and contact your list of external agencies and provision of support services. Clarify contact, support offered, cost and estimated waiting list.	
7. Assessing, tracking and recording safeguarding concerns and interventions	• Each week have a line management meeting with the MHFA and/or pastoral team to discuss safeguarding issues, students at risk and strategies for support, overseeing interventions and establishing links with external agencies and professionals. Ensure individual student support mental wellbeing plan is filled in and parents are contacted.	
Additional points I want to add that are specific to my school		

Summer Term 3b	Strategic focus	Some evidence of being embedded	Fully embedded and evidenced
1. Leadership, strategy and governance	• Focus on the termly planner in this book: leadership and strategy; staff support and wellbeing; student support and wellbeing; staff professional development and learning on mental health; working with parents and carers; working with external services. Based on how you have RAGed yourself this year (red/amber/green[7]), build in objectives that have yet to be fully embedded.		
	• Meet with the SLT and evaluate what still needs to be fully embedded and write in targets that will enable your school to build a whole-school culture of mental health and wellbeing into the forthcoming year's SPD.		
	• Meet with the DSL and review safeguarding and mental health and the process from making a referral to triage to follow-up to measuring impact. Review what still needs to be improved. Based on these results, plan inset training days for the following year.		
	• Review progress of the mental health award. How many of the criteria have you met so far? Prepare for an assessment visit to assess whether your school is bronze, silver or gold.		
2. Staff professional development for mental health and wellbeing	• Train staff in the mental health briefing for Healthy Eating Awareness Week in June (see Appendix 1).		
	• Meet the Staff Wellbeing Action Group (SWAGS). Plan into the school diary or planner, as part of directed, not additional, time, SWAG meetings for the following year.		
3. Student mental wellbeing and identifying students at risk	• Meet the mental health ambassadors weekly, and supervise their safeguarding.		
	• Identify and review the list of students at risk and oversee strategies for support and interventions, establishing links with external agencies and professionals. Ensure the individual student support mental wellbeing plan is written.		
	• Review the impact of lunchtime spaces such as the wellbeing zone.		
	• Prepare vulnerable students for the holidays.		

---

7   Red amber green reporting is essentially a traffic light system that tells you that red statuses are incomplete or still need to be addressed, amber signals some progress has been made but more needs to be done and green means that everything is on track and on the way to being embedded.

Curriculum area	Actions			
4. Curriculum planning and resources	• Review the mental health curriculum for Summer Term 2b. • Plan lessons to coincide with Healthy Eating Awareness Week in June. • Plan lessons to coincide with Volunteers' Week.[8] This is a chance to celebrate and say thank you for the fantastic contribution millions of volunteers make across the UK. It takes place 1–7 June every year and is an opportunity to celebrate volunteering in all its diversity.			
5. Working with parents and the wider community	• Update the website on National Awareness days. Send out articles in the newsletter; record podcasts on healthy eating.			
6. Working with external agencies and provision of support services	• Book in speakers for assemblies and inset days on stress awareness, eating disorders, healthy eating (refer to 'National Awareness Days' at the end of this book to see what is coming up). • Review and update your register and contact your list of external agencies and providers of support services working with particular students. Clarify contact, support offered, cost and estimated waiting list.			
7. Assessing, tracking and recording safeguarding concerns and interventions	• Each week have a line management meeting with the MHFA and/or pastoral team to discuss safeguarding issues, students at risk and strategies for support, overseeing interventions and establishing links with external agencies and professionals. • Ensure the individual student support mental wellbeing plan is filled in and parents are contacted. • Plan a strategy to prepare and support vulnerable students for the holidays.			
Additional points I want to add that are specific to my school				

Chapter 13

Weekly Planner

AUTUMN TERM 1A
Week 1

Purpose of the week: What is mental health and why does my role in a school matter?

My goals:

- ☐ Set performance management targets in line with the DMHL. Prioritize any training you would like this year for your own CPD. Take a look at the suggestions in Chapter 8.

- ☐ Prepare for World Suicide Prevention Day coming up on 10 September. Visit the website for ideas,[1] and look at the safety plan they offer. All staff will need warning about this in advance so that it is not 'triggering' for any who have experience of this.

- ☐ Inform staff of the Staff Wellbeing Action Group (SWAGS) and proposed meeting dates for the year. Make sure new staff are informed about this proactive group and encouraged to join.

- ☐ Inform the MHFA of your line management slot with them each week.

- ☐ Meet with the MHFA to discuss safeguarding issues, students at risk and strategies for support, overseeing interventions and establishing links with external agencies and professionals. Ensure the individual student support mental wellbeing plan is filled in and parents are contacted (see Appendix 5)

- ☐ On the first day of inset introduce yourself to staff and signpost the staff wellbeing room, SWAG and the reason for your role.

- ☐ _____

- ☐ _____

- ☐ _____

---

1   www.stayingsafe.net

What worked well, and what would you do differently?

Remember that self-care is an essential part of my daily routine.

- I am grateful for: _____

  _____

  _____

- My mental wellbeing action for this week is to ensure I _____

  _____

  _____

- What I am currently reading/listening to: _____

  _____

  _____

Summary for Week 1

1. This week is about putting this role on your performance management agenda. Quickly identify the training you would like or need and put in a request for the CPD.

2. It is also about raising awareness of your role. Ask the DSL in July to make sure the DMHL role and the referral procedures are itemized in the first inset day back. When photos and names are released of the DSL, make sure photos are also taken of the DMHL and MHFA. They are all part of the safeguarding team.

3. Profiling the SWAG and its function: it might be worth getting SWAG meetings put in the official school calendar, so they are built into directed time and are not seen as an additional extra.

4. Meeting the MHFA and being ready to support students straight away. When meeting the MHFA make it a weekly slot. Get it placed on the online timetable and booked out so you both can't be used for cover or for other meetings. It's worth putting together a meeting template for meeting the MHFA as time is short, with much that is needed to get through.

Week 2

Purpose of the week: Setting up clear signposting. Let staff and students know where to go, when to go and who they can see for mental health and support.

My goals:

☐ Write or review mental health policies or guidance documents for staff and student mental health support. Submit to the SLT or governors for ratification.

☐ 10 September is World Suicide Prevention Day. Deliver assemblies and create mental health or tutor-themed lessons.[2]

☐ Have a meeting with the SLT to discuss strategy. Advise joining a mental health award scheme and work through bronze, silver or gold criteria.

☐ Organize the staff rota that lists who is on duty in the different spaces in the student wellbeing zone at lunchtimes. Ensure signage is set up and clear about the function of each of the rooms (see Appendix 1).

☐ Prepare a training programme for the mental wellbeing ambassadors. Book a venue and trainer. Training is to be delivered by staff MHFA ambassadors (see Chapter 12, 'Harness the Power of Peer Mentoring' in *Mental Health and Wellbeing Handbook for Schools*).[3] Half a day training with a follow-up hour is suggested.

☐ Meet with the MHFA to discuss safeguarding issues, students at risk and strategies for support, overseeing interventions and establishing links with external agencies and professionals. Ensure the individual student support mental wellbeing plan is filled in and parents are contacted (see Appendix 5).

☐ _____

☐ _____

☐ _____

2   Also check out https://stayingsafe.net/youngpeople
3   Erasmus, C. (2019) *Mental Health and Wellbeing Handbook for Schools: Transforming Mental Health Support on a Budget*. London: Jessica Kingsley Publishers.

What worked well, and what would you do differently?

Remember that self-care is an essential part of my daily routine.

- I am grateful for: _____

  _____

  _____

- My mental wellbeing action for this week is to ensure I _____

  _____

  _____

- What I am currently reading/listening to: _____

  _____

  _____

Summary for Week 2

1. This week is about setting up adult and student mentor support in the wellbeing zone. This includes ensuring clear signposting. Let students know where to go, when to go and who they will see for mental health and support.

2. The policies or guidance documents are essential as they ensure that all staff can be clear about signs to look out for, referral procedures, people to contact and due diligence that needs to be practised by all staff.

3. Setting up the school with rolling out a mental health award means the DMHL will have a mandate when rolling out a whole-school culture of mental wellbeing. It legitimizes initiatives for whole-staff buy-in and can be delivered later and rolled out by a collective staff group, like SWAGS.

Week 3

Purpose of the week: Auditing, training and networking.

My goals:

- ☐ Finish writing or reviewing mental health policies, referral forms and individual student support mental wellbeing plan pro formas.

- ☐ Working with the SLT, secure morning mental health briefings with staff for the course of the year (see Appendix 1 for ideas).

- ☐ Complete a self-audit of the school's mental health award. Make a note of all that your school offers students and staff in terms of support with mental health.

- ☐ Make contact with your local consortium, mental health forums or hubs. Put your name down and join the debate so you can agree a wellbeing protocol for your whole community and be aware of how to work with the working mental health parties.

- ☐ Train the mental wellbeing ambassadors. Training to be delivered by staff MHFA ambassadors (for a basic breakdown of peer ambassador training programmes read Chapter 12, 'Harness the Power of Peer Mentoring', in *Mental Health and Wellbeing Handbook for Schools*).[4]

- ☐ Meet with the MHFA to discuss safeguarding issues, students at risk and strategies for support, overseeing interventions and establishing links with external agencies and professionals. Ensure the individual student support mental wellbeing plan is filled in and parents are contacted (see Appendix 5).

- ☐ _____

  _____

- ☐ _____

  _____

- ☐ _____

  _____

---

4   Erasmus, C. (2019) *Mental Health and Wellbeing Handbook for Schools: Transforming Mental Health Support on a Budget.* London: Jessica Kingsley Publishers.

What worked well, and what would you do differently?

Remember that self-care is an essential part of my daily routine.

- I am grateful for: _____

  _____

  _____

- My mental wellbeing action for this week is to ensure I _____

  _____

  _____

- What I am currently reading/listening to: _____

  _____

  _____

Summary for Week 3

1. This week is about auditing, training and networking. It's also about connecting and building the network within and outside the school community.

2. The morning briefings for staff are so that you can drip-feed vital working practice with staff, from mindfulness to de-escalation techniques to listening without judgement and non-directive therapy to supporting and staff looking after themselves.

3. Training the mental health ambassadors is vital so that you have them ready to go straight from the start. Get them badges and make sure the presentation is official and has the gravitas needed to show these peers are hugely respected for what they are offering. Arrange a meeting once a week so you can 'hot potato' anything that is of concern to them to you and so you can ensure they feel valued and that their own mental health is supported.

Week 4

Purpose of the week: Utilize the wealth of online resources with readymade assembly plans, lessons and audio-visual resources.

My goals:

- 10 October is World Mental Health Day. Plan and finalize activities, videos, lesson plans for assemblies and lessons. Visit websites such as the Anna Freud National Centre for Children and Families resources page for schools and colleges[5] and the NHS page 'Every mind matters'.[6]

- ☐ Get your school subscribed as a paid-up member of the PSHE Association[7] for a wealth of lesson plans and resources.

- ☐ Introduce journaling for students who start to show early signs of concern. A great resource for journaling is published by Butterfly Print.[8]

- ☐ Visit the Depressed Cake Shop[9] cake sale for great ideas on holding a cake sale with a mental health theme.

- ☐ Meet with wellbeing ambassadors and the MHFA to discuss ideas for developing the different parts of the wellbeing zone (see Appendix 1 and the section on self-referral spaces).

- ☐ Discuss the results of school self-audit (part of the criteria for most mental health awards) with the SLT. What can stay, go or be revamped?

- ☐ Meet with the MHFA to discuss safeguarding issues, students at risk and strategies for support, overseeing interventions and establishing links with external agencies and professionals. Ensure the individual student support mental wellbeing plan is filled in and parents are contacted (see Appendix 5).

- ☐ _____

    _____

- ☐ _____

    _____

- ☐ _____

    _____

---

5 www.annafreud.org/schools-and-colleges/resources
6 NHS (no date) 'Every mind matters.' Available at: www.nhs.uk/oneyou/every-mind-matters
7 www.pshe-association.org.uk
8 www.butterflyprint.co.uk/product-category/mental-health/mental-health-journals
9 https://depressedcakeshop.com

What worked well, and what would you do differently?

Remember that self-care is an essential part of my daily routine.

- I am grateful for: _____

  _____

  _____

- My mental wellbeing action for this week is to ensure I _____

  _____

  _____

- What I am currently reading/listening to: _____

  _____

  _____

Summary for Week 4

1. This week is about utilizing the wealth of online resources with readymade assembly plans, lessons and audio-visual resources for World Mental Health Day coming up in October.

2. Engage students and remind them of the support available to them at lunchtimes and being able to pop in and visit the wellbeing zone.

3. It is also about getting the students to lead in raising awareness in the wellbeing zone and in assemblies, which can have a greater impact.

Week 5

Purpose of the week: Continuing the conversation – time to change, time to talk.

My goals:

☐ Send out two approved mental health and wellbeing guidance documents or policies – one for supporting staff mental wellbeing and another on supporting student mental wellbeing.

☐ Visit the NHS mental health apps,[10] and investigate introducing a mental health app to staff and students outside of school hours. Once you have chosen an app, ensure there is an assembly for the younger students on what the app is and how it can be used to support young people, where it can be downloaded and how. (Make sure that a letter has gone out to parents first, introducing the benefits of your choice of mental health and wellbeing app.)

☐ Deliver a mental health briefing to all staff about the staff referral procedure for mental health concerns.

☐ Contact the local Rotary Club and their Youth Services section to see about sourcing funding so, for example, an after-school cookery club can take place to support vulnerable young people and young carers. Look for local charities and organizations that are keen to get involved in the local school community.

☐ Meet with the MHFA to discuss safeguarding issues, students at risk and strategies for support, overseeing interventions and establishing links with external agencies and professionals. Ensure the individual student support mental wellbeing plan is filled in and parents are contacted (see Appendix 5).

☐ _____
_____

☐ _____
_____

☐ _____
_____

---

10   www.nhs.uk/apps-library/category/mental-health/?page=1

What worked well, and what would you do differently?

Remember that self-care is an essential part of my daily routine.

- I am grateful for: _____

  _____

  _____

- My mental wellbeing action for this week is to ensure I _____

  _____

  _____

- What I am currently reading/listening to: _____

  _____

  _____

Summary for Week 5

1. This week is about getting the information out there to all staff. Have they read the student and staff mental health and wellbeing guidance document? How can you evidence this has been done? Do they know where to find it?

2. Try and ensure that the school builds relationships with local community projects, voluntary organizations and networks.

3. Make use of technology such as mental health and wellbeing apps to try and support young people and their parents at home as well.

Week 6

Purpose of the week: Train staff, raise awareness and connect with parents.

My goals:

- ☐ Plan inset training for staff on how to set up a safe classroom when teaching mental health lessons (see Appendix 1).

- ☐ Review mental health lessons for the second half of term for all year groups.

- ☐ Regarding the mental health award objectives, prompt the head teacher to agree a date when the staff wellbeing survey will be sent out.

- ☐ Train mental health ambassadors in mindfulness in their meeting once a week.

- ☐ Suggest to mental health ambassadors that they start writing a column for the school newsletter.

- ☐ Meet anti-bullying ambassadors to start planning for Anti-Bullying Week.

- ☐ Arrange with the SLT that an email will be sent to parents about supporting teenage mental health at home and when to be concerned.

- ☐ Meet with the MHFA to discuss safeguarding issues, students at risk and strategies for support, overseeing interventions and establishing links with external agencies and professionals. Ensure the individual student support mental wellbeing plan is filled in and parents are contacted (see Appendix 5).

- ☐ _____

      _____

- ☐ _____

      _____

- ☐ _____

      _____

What worked well, and what would you do differently?

Remember that self-care is an essential part of my daily routine.

- I am grateful for: _____

  _____

  _____

- My mental wellbeing action for this week is to ensure I _____

  _____

  _____

- What I am currently reading/listening to: _____

  _____

  _____

Summary for Week 6

1. This week is about continuing to raise awareness for staff, parents and students, hence the inset training to be delivered.

2. It is also about the mental health and wellbeing ambassadors' voices being heard in the newsletter.

3. A good idea for connecting with parents might be to use pre-recorded podcasts or YouTube videos instead of trying to get them all into a hall after a long day, or even a pre-recorded PowerPoint lesson. We live in an age of audio-visual digital platforms, so let's harness them. Make sure you are always letting parents know where they can get additional support and how they can support their young people.

Week 7

Purpose of the week: Raise concern, triage, refer for intervention, track, measure impact, repeat.

My goals:

- ☐ Follow up, attend or review your own CPD training. What have you completed? What do you still need to do? Hopefully it can all form part of your Performance Management targets.

- ☐ Review the list of students referred through CPOMS[11] (a software solution for monitoring safeguarding, wellbeing and all pastoral issues), and examine strategies your school is putting into place. Make or update a list of the vulnerable students on your radar. Ensure you plan outcomes for each student (see Appendix 3).

- ☐ Review the staff who have been working closely with vulnerable students. Do they need supervision? Ensure that supervision is offered before the half-term holidays so they can pass on their concerns and not take them with them on their holidays.

- ☐ Meet with the DSL and review the half term just gone. Were any concerns raised? Examine the impact of interventions carried out. What was the impact? How are the DSL and DMHL teams working together? What can be streamlined?

- ☐ Prepare the mental health curriculum for the next half term. Remind teachers about how to ensure their classrooms are safe spaces to have conversations that protect, educate and support all our young people (see Appendix 1 for suggested training).

- ☐ Prepare a draft for the staff survey that will address mental wellbeing and workload. If you are using some online platforms such as EduPod,[12] they will provide the validated survey. Otherwise, you can also look at TES.[13]

- ☐ _____

- ☐ _____

- ☐ _____

---

11   www.cpoms.co.uk
12   www.myedupod.com
13   www.tes.com/for-schools/empower/staff-pulse

What worked well, and what would you do differently?

Remember that self-care is an essential part of my daily routine.

- I am grateful for: _____

  _____

  _____

- My mental wellbeing action for this week is to ensure I _____

  _____

  _____

- What I am currently reading/listening to: _____

  _____

  _____

Summary for Week 7

1. This week is about making sure that once a concern is raised, it is effectively triaged, referred, tracked, measured against realistic outcomes and all the relevant data is where it should be.

2. It is also vital that staff who work with the most vulnerable students are offered and given supervision. See Chapter 2, 'Working with the Designated Safeguarding Lead and Supervision', for information on how to support yourself and your staff.

3. It might also be necessary to ensure the DMHL receives training so they can offer supervision to internal staff.

AUTUMN TERM 1B
Week 1

Purpose of the week: Train staff and prepare the school for Anti-Bullying Week and make stakeholders aware of the links of bullying and its impact on people's mental health.

My goals:

☐ This half term generally comes with an inset day. Request 45 minutes to train all staff (see Appendix 1 for suggested training, although note that each school will be at a different point).

☐ Meet with the anti-bullying ambassadors to discuss the national anti-bullying theme for the year. What assemblies do they want to present? Ideas for activities can range from drama shows in assembly to Wearing Odd Socks days.

☐ Remind staff and students of activities at lunchtime running in the wellbeing zone.

☐ Meet with the head teacher to finalize the draft for the staff survey that will address mental wellbeing and workload. The school may also want to look at the Department for Education 'School workload reduction toolkit' and use it as well, or parts of it.[14]

☐ Meet with student wellbeing ambassadors and talk about stress points in the term, and anxieties that are being shared by other students. November or December tends to see revision programmes and mock exam preparation and life–work balance starts to get out of kilter, leading to increased anxiety amongst students. Speak to staff and the SLT if the school needs to review how it is ensuring a culture of life–work balance for both staff and students.

☐ Meet with the MHFA to discuss safeguarding issues, students at risk and strategies for support, overseeing interventions and establishing links with external agencies and professionals. Ensure the individual student support mental wellbeing plan is filled in and parents are contacted (see Appendix 5).

☐ _____

☐ _____

☐ _____

---

14   www.gov.uk/guidance/school-workload-reduction-toolkit

What worked well, and what would you do differently?

Remember that self-care is an essential part of my daily routine.

- I am grateful for: _____

  _____

  _____

- My mental wellbeing action for this week is to ensure I _____

  _____

  _____

- What I am currently reading/listening to: _____

  _____

  _____

Summary for Week 1

1. This week is about profiling bullying and its impact on people's mental health and to engage the anti-bullying student ambassadors, so they are leading the campaign within the school. A school culture where both staff and students see themselves as upstanders (someone who stands up to bullying as opposed to being a bystander) can make a huge difference to everyone's mental wellbeing.

2. I suggest having a staff member with passion and energy as the anti-bullying coordinator so they can motivate all stakeholders to get involved. The first term is generally the longest term of the year, so tensions will start to loom as mock exam pressures start to feature. It's important that the DMHL is keeping an eye on life–work balance for teachers and students, and to ensure lunchtimes are for recharging and not for catch-up lessons or meetings.

Week 2

Purpose of the week: To raise awareness on the need for life–school balance for both staff and students and to engage the students in strategies for coping.

My goals:

☐ Meet the wellbeing ambassadors. Continue the discussion about strategies and stress points. Use resources from Young Minds[15] such as the butterfly template, which allows students to identify what they need to do in their school work (and possible worries) and the things they do (or could do) to get a good balance in the run-up to tests or exams, and also the Stress Buster Timetable.[16]

☐ Prepare the staff and student wellbeing survey to be placed on SurveyMonkey or Microsoft Forms for distribution early next month.

☐ #familyMH5aday campaign (see Appendix 6) for Year 7 students: arrange an assembly for the launch of the #familyMH5aday campaign and all the activities that the students will do.

☐ Prepare a letter for parents on the value of the #familyMH5aday campaign.

☐ Announce in a briefing that all faculties should meet for lunch at least one day this week. Encourage a day next week where faculties join with another faculty. It's important we get staff connecting and sharing. See #teacher5aday[17] for plenty more ideas.

☐ Meet with the MHFA to discuss safeguarding issues, students at risk and strategies for support, overseeing interventions.

☐ _____

☐ _____

☐ _____

15   https://youngminds.org.uk/media/2979/butterfly-of-balance.pdf
16   https://youngminds.org.uk/resources/school-resources/stress-buster-timetable-for-exam-time
17   https://martynreah.wordpress.com/2014/12/06/teacher5aday

What worked well, and what would you do differently?

Remember that self-care is an essential part of my daily routine.

- I am grateful for: _____

  _____

  _____

- My mental wellbeing action for this week is to ensure I _____

  _____

  _____

- What I am currently reading/listening to: _____

  _____

  _____

Summary for Week 2

1. This week is about raising awareness on the need for life–school balance for both staff and students and engaging students with strategies for coping. Some of the students' stress-busting ideas could include breakfast clubs, mindfulness, listening to music and meeting a mentor. Sometimes it's just making sure students keep some free time in their timetables to keep a healthy revision–life balance.

2. Listen to staff and student voices through the mental wellbeing survey.

3. Engage younger students and the family with #familyMH5aday.

Week 3

Purpose of the week: Running Anti-Bullying Week in November, listening to student voices and measuring impact.

My goals:

- ☐ Deliver a presentation to Year 7 on #familyMH5aday (this campaign runs in the five weeks in the build-up to Christmas and works well with Year 7 and primary school students; see Appendix 6). Send an email to parents.

- ☐ Deliver scheduled anti-bullying assemblies and always link bullying to the impact it also has on mental health. I always stress rights and responsibilities – we all have the right to feel safe in our school, but with that right comes the responsibility to be an upstander and role model.

- ☐ Share on social media and connect with leading charities such as The Diana Award[18] and the Anti-Bullying Alliance.[19]

- ☐ The drama department deliver an anti-bullying play they have devised along the national theme.

- ☐ Run an anti-bullying cake sale and poster competition.

- ☐ Roll out an anti-bullying survey in school to see what students know about the support in the school and whether they feel procedures are in place for dealing with bullying.

- ☐ Review how the anti-bullying reports are being filed, for example, handwritten or emailed to tutors to follow up on, tracked, etc. Record the footfall of students visiting the anti-bullying room.

- ☐ Prepare an anti-bullying report for governors.

- ☐ Meet with the MHFA to discuss safeguarding issues, students at risk and strategies for support.

- ☐ _____

- ☐ _____

- ☐ _____

---

18 https://diana-award.org.uk/anti-bullying
19 www.anti-bullyingalliance.org.uk

What worked well, and what would you do differently?

Remember that self-care is an essential part of my daily routine.

- I am grateful for: _____

  _____

  _____

- My mental wellbeing action for this week is to ensure I ____

  _____

  _____

- What I am currently reading/listening to: _____

  _____

  _____

Summary for Week 3

1. This week is about overseeing Anti-Bullying Week and ensuring all the plans come together. Powerful assemblies with students performing improvised drama plays exploring bullying online and in school are always popular, and running Be Kind campaigns really helps put a positive spin on what we expect in our schools. It's also a good opportunity to listen to student voices and to measure the impact of your school's initiatives and allow the data to inform your development.

2. This data will prove to be very powerful when reporting back to governors on the initiatives of the anti-bullying ambassadors, the anti-bullying room, whether the number of reports have decreased or increased, what types of bullying are dominant in your school and what you are going to do about it.

3. It's really important that all anti-bullying reports are filed in a secure place and each report is tracked and there is a follow-up for both students and in some cases the parents too.

Week 4

Purpose of the week: Research into the viability of getting a therapy dog.

My goals:

- ☐ Research therapy dogs online.[20]

- ☐ Present the idea to the governors. Why get a therapy dog? Show them case studies and evidence-based practice.

- ☐ Work on a policy for a therapy dog.[21]

- ☐ Prepare a draft proposal for the SLT.

- ☐ Meet with the MHFA to discuss safeguarding issues, students at risk and strategies for support, overseeing interventions and establishing links with external agencies and professionals. Ensure the individual student support mental wellbeing plan is filled in and parents are contacted (see Appendix 5). Review risk assessments for the young person.

- ☐ _____

  _____

- ☐ _____

  _____

- ☐ _____

  _____

20 www.tdn.org.uk/schools/; Grové, C. and Henderson, L. (2018) 'Therapy dogs can help reduce student stress, anxiety and improve school attendance.' *The Conversation*, 19 March. Available at: http://theconversation.com/therapy-dogs-can-help-reduce-student-stress-anxiety-and-improve-school-attendance-93073. Case study: www.kingshillschool.org.uk/Pet-Therapy
21 See, for example, https://hazel-oak.co.uk/wp-content/uploads/2018/02/School-Dog-Policy.pdf

What worked well, and what would you do differently?

Remember that self-care is an essential part of my daily routine.

- I am grateful for: _____

_____

_____

- My mental wellbeing action for this week is to ensure I _____

_____

_____

- What I am currently reading/listening to: _____

_____

_____

Summary for Week 4

1. Research has shown that having a dog in school can help with managing emotional strategies for coping with stress and anxiety, interpersonal skills, attendance, behaviour, confidence and self-esteem, teaching responsibility and respect for all life, and motivating children who are often less attentive. The students also learn about responsibility, caring and sharing when helping each other take care of a dog at school.

2. This week is about setting up proposals and investigating structures into the possibility of getting a therapy dog.

3. It is important to understand the following: costs, who will own the dog and manage the dog at school, insurance, assessing the risks, the right training, getting governors and parents on board, preparing the children and staff on conduct around the dog with a list of dos and don'ts, and having a timetable for the dog with rest periods away from students.

Week 5

Purpose of the week: Review what you have set up, check if it is in line with the school inspection framework and prepare to gather qualitative data.

My goals:

☐ Familiarize yourself with the school inspection framework and how it links to mental health and wellbeing for staff and students.[22]

☐ Review the availability of information about mental health and wellbeing and support on your school website and on posters around the school. Where is the information if a teacher, parent or student wants to look?

☐ Review or set up a wellbeing support email account and address. This means students can email a mental health concern rather than having to see someone face to face. It's important the email is directed to someone who will definitely check it every day.

☐ Review safeguarding and mental health. How has mental health featured in the safeguarding policy?

☐ Review mental wellbeing policy or guidance documents for students and staff. Reflect on what you will add or change for next year.

☐ Review the impact of safeguarding and mental health support; consider surveys, face-to-face questions or forums with pupils, parents, staff and governors. Create and get ready to conduct this research.

☐ Prepare to analyse data.

☐ Meet with the MHFA to discuss safeguarding issues, students at risk and strategies for support, overseeing interventions and establishing links with external agencies and professionals.

☐ _____

☐ _____

☐ _____

---

22 Ofsted (2005) *School Inspection Handbook: Handbook for Inspecting Schools in England Under Section 5 of the Education Act 2005*. Available at: https://assets.publishing.service.gov.uk/government/uploads/system/uploads/attachment_data/file/843108/School_inspection_handbook_-_section_5.pdf

What worked well, and what would you do differently?

Remember that self-care is an essential part of my daily routine.

- I am grateful for: _____

_____

_____

- My mental wellbeing action for this week is to ensure I _____

_____

_____

- What I am currently reading/listening to: _____

_____

_____

Summary for Week 5

1. Familiarize yourself with the latest Ofsted framework and how it pertains to mental health and wellbeing for staff and students.

2. This week is about the DMHL's responsibility to also make sure that key policy documents and information about the structures and support available are all clearly visible on the school website. This is so parents, staff and students can access the necessary information as and when they are ready.

3. Sending out the surveys will help ensure you are being vigilant about listening to staff concerns about workload and wellbeing and the experience of school pupils, and whether they feel supported and their mental health needs are being met. This directly links up with the latest updates in the new Ofsted framework.[23]

---

23 https://assets.publishing.service.gov.uk/government/uploads/system/uploads/attachment_data/file/843108/School_inspection_handbook_-_section_5.pdf

Week 6

Purpose of the week: Review training, referrals, safeguarding risks, interventions and outcomes.

My goals:

☐ Review the effectiveness of training delivered in the school. What still needs to happen? (See Appendix 1.)

☐ Review newly qualified teachers' (NQTs) and new members of staff's understanding of mental health, safeguarding and reporting, and arrange to deliver top-up CPD. We often forget to train the new staff and NQTs who missed the inset delivered at the start of the year.

☐ Review the Term 2 curriculum for mental health.

☐ Conduct student wellbeing surveys you have prepared in previous weeks.

☐ Review any referrals staff have made about students and safeguarding risks and interventions taking place. Update your records and start to measure impact against agreed outcomes (see Appendix 3).

☐ Review and quality assure external agencies working with your students.

☐ Review the breakdown of mental health challenges facing the young people in your school. Isolate key areas of concern and plan workshops and inset days for your staff for the rest of this year and next, for example: self-harm; eating disorders; suicide ideation; anxiety and stress related to exams and revision.

☐ Meet with the MHFA to discuss safeguarding issues, students at risk and strategies for support, overseeing interventions and establishing links with external agencies and professionals. Ensure the individual student support mental wellbeing plan is filled in and parents are contacted (see Appendix 5). Review risk assessments for the young person.

☐ _____

_____

☐ _____

_____

☐ _____

_____

What worked well, and what would you do differently?

Remember that self-care is an essential part of my daily routine.

- I am grateful for: _____

  _____

  _____

- My mental wellbeing action for this week is to ensure I _____

  _____

  _____

- What I am currently reading/listening to: _____

  _____

  _____

Summary for Week 6

1. This week is an essential part of the DMHL's role to ensure that all staff members know when and how to record concerns about a child's mental wellbeing, however small or apparently insignificant they may seem. The DMHL should ensure that all NEW staff members are also given appropriate induction and refresher training and are supervised appropriately in carrying out these arrangements; hence, reviewing it this week is vital, so no one has missed out on the training.

2. It is also the DMHL's role to work closely with the DSL to maintain a stand-alone file for children with child protection or welfare concerns. Some of these young people will have very clear mental health challenges, so placing the right support in place for them is vital.

3. This information must be clearly tracked, risk assessments updated and saved, and outcomes be measurable.

Week 7

Purpose of the week: Collate results of the survey for staff and students.

My goals:

- ☐ Start to collate the results for the staff wellbeing survey. Using an online platform like SurveyMonkey or Microsoft Forms will definitely help, or some mental health online solutions such as EduPod[24] provide a readymade survey for both staff and students within the package, and they collate the results.

- ☐ Start to collate the results for the student wellbeing survey.

- ☐ Follow up with Year 7s and tutors on the #familyMH5aday campaign that is still running.

- ☐ Arrange a time to meet the SWAGS before Christmas.

- ☐ Plan staff wellbeing events like Secret Santa, Christmas Jumper Day, Christmas Bake Off, a staff pantomime or Christmas lip sync music videos.

- ☐ Present an assembly on giving and the links of giving and volunteering and the impact it can have on our mental health. Ask the mental wellbeing ambassadors to present these to the junior years. Start a shoebox collection for those who are less fortunate and homeless people on the back of this presentation.

- ☐ Work closely with the head of Year 11 to ensure that there is a balance in the language we use in the mock exam period so we ensure that academic excellence is not focused on at the expense of mental health and wellbeing.

- ☐ Meet with the MHFA to discuss safeguarding issues, students at risk and strategies for support, overseeing interventions and establishing links with external agencies and professionals. Ensure the individual student support mental wellbeing plan is filled in and parents are contacted (see Appendix 5). Review risk assessments.

- ☐ _____

- ☐ _____

- ☐ _____

---

24 www.myedupod.com

What worked well, and what would you do differently?

Remember that self-care is an essential part of my daily routine.

- I am grateful for: _____

  _____

  _____

- My mental wellbeing action for this week is to ensure I _____

  _____

  _____

- What I am currently reading/listening to: _____

  _____

  _____

Summary for Week 7

1. This week is about ensuring the staff and young people feel heard and listened to.

2. Holding assemblies to champion the value of giving and its links with mental health is always very topical and relevant at this time of year.

3. Staff tend to fall ill in this term and really struggle with the workload, so ensure that emails are kept to a minimum and a stream of little gestures is made – ensuring a sense of community and mindfulness towards each other. This can range from Secret Santa, Christmas Jumper Day, a day off in lieu of twilight insets so staff can do their own Christmas shopping, and staff wellbeing advent calendars.

Week 8

Purpose of the week: Build calm and support before Christmas.

My goals:

☐ Review children who will be a safeguarding concern over the Christmas period. Work closely with the DSL on setting up support structures for them when school is closed. See the excellent template provided by Dr Pooky Knightsmith that teachers or the MHFA or DMHL can use.[25]

☐ Another great resource, Winter Wellbeing, can be found on the Heads Together website.[26] It has exercises and techniques to help children feel calm and release energy, wellbeing games and activities for pupils, tools, tips, advice and videos for supporting staff wellbeing, and a Wheel of Life activity to reflect on how satisfied you are with different parts of your life – you can then think about how to improve certain areas that you find more challenging. A good idea would be to run an assembly on this, talking about the strategies. Share with staff and parents too.

☐ Work with a local charity and arrange to get the young people to deliver gift boxes and give up their time to do something that keeps the spirit of kindness and giving high on the agenda, such as Christmas boxes for homeless people or visiting a residential care home and singing Christmas songs and laying on a Christmas tea.

☐ Ensure staff are properly rested and there are events happening before the Christmas break to support staff wellbeing.

☐ Meet with the MHFA to discuss safeguarding issues, students at risk and strategies for support.

☐ _____

☐ _____

☐ _____

25 Knightsmith, P. (2017) 'How to help vulnerable pupils prepare for the summer holidays.' SecEd, 7 June. Available at: www.sec-ed.co.uk/best-practice/how-to-help-vulnerable-pupils-prepare-for-the-summer-holidays

26 www.mentallyhealthyschools.org.uk/media/1927/winter-wellbeing-toolkit.pdf?utm_source=facebook&utm_medium=social&utm_campaign=winterwellbeing_2019&utm_term=headstogether&utm_content=toolkit

What worked well, and what would you do differently?

Remember that self-care is an essential part of my daily routine.

- I am grateful for: _____

  _____

  _____

- My mental wellbeing action for this week is to ensure I _____

  _____

  _____

- What I am currently reading/listening to: _____

  _____

  _____

Summary for Week 8

1. This week is about how to help support vulnerable students with mental health challenges over the holidays (see Appendix 1 for interventions that can be put in place).

2. Make sure the SLT provide opportunities for staff to prioritize their wellbeing. These can range from avoiding long evenings with meetings and after-school meetings, a staff Christmas social, Secret Santa, providing all staff with a Christmas breakfast and dependency days so staff can attend their own children's nativity plays.

3. Arrange to support a local charity with gift boxes to keep the spirit of giving and kindness high on the agenda.

Week 9

Purpose of the week: Prepare to reboot, and then let it go...

My goals:

- ☐ Prepare a 'You said, We did' response for the staff survey. It would be good to roll this out in the new term – a fresh start for a fresh year.

- ☐ Send an email notifying staff of the mental health lessons taking place next term. Proofread all lessons and remind staff on the inset day you delivered about setting up safe classrooms and enabling 'safe' discussions and the use of the 'Ask it' basket (see Appendix 1).

- ☐ Plan for Children's Mental Health Week, which generally takes place in the first few weeks of February.

- ☐ The Time to Talk Day also takes place in early February.

- ☐ Collate #familyMH5aday and award house points to students who took part in the build-up to Christmas.

- ☐ Meet the SWAGS and sum up three positives and three suggestions for reducing workload.

- ☐ Enjoy Secret Santa, Christmas Jumper Day, Christmas Bake Off, staff pantomime or Christmas lip sync music videos.

- ☐ Meet with wellbeing ambassadors and introduce the concept of slowing things down and being more mindful and aware and what is self-compassion.

- ☐ Review children who will be a safeguarding concern over the Christmas period. Work closely with the DSL on setting up support structures for them when school is closed.

- ☐ Finally, check who needs supervision before the Christmas break in terms of staff, the MHFA and, of course, the DSL and DMHL (see Chapters 2 and 9).

- ☐ _____
  _____

- ☐ _____
  _____

- ☐ _____
  _____

What worked well, and what would you do differently?

Remember that self-care is an essential part of my daily routine.

- I am grateful for: _____

  _____

  _____

- My mental wellbeing action for this week is to ensure I _____

  _____

  _____

- What I am currently reading/listening to: _____

  _____

  _____

Summary for Week 9

1. This week is about enjoying the festive period but also keeping a watchful eye out for students who are feeling anxious about the holidays.

2. The role of the DMHL is about safeguarding and supporting students and staff when it comes to mental health, but it is widely regarded that 'mental health is everyone's business', so, in the run-up to Christmas, it's a perfect opportunity to engage all staff and all students in a wave of kindness and giving to each other and to the wider community.

3. Support from the top is key. If the SLT champion ideas to help with staff wellbeing, such as Secret SLT missions of kindness to *all* staff and secret buddy missions, it can make a real difference in the longest term of the year in the build-up to Christmas.

SPRING TERM 2A
Week 1

Purpose of the week: What we are doing as a school to get involved in Children's Mental Health Week.

My goals:

☐ Finalize the 'You said, We did' response for the staff survey. Plan a date for delivery or feedback.

☐ Check in that lessons with mental health and relationships and sex education are being delivered. Chat to students about the topic and lessons being delivered. Get a feel for how the lessons are being received, holding informal focus groups.

☐ Meet the student wellbeing ambassadors and plan what they would like to do in your wellbeing zone. Plan for Children's Mental Health Week.[27]

☐ Research the Time to Talk Day[28] in early February. Plan to meet the SWAGS to see how staff can embrace this.

☐ Present a mental health briefing on a topic that *all* staff could benefit from knowing about, such as self-harm, anxiety, panic attacks, supporting young carers, etc.

☐ Meet with the MHFA to discuss safeguarding issues, students at risk and strategies for support, overseeing interventions and establishing links with external agencies and professionals. Ensure the individual student support mental wellbeing plan is filled in and parents are contacted (see Appendix 5). Review risk assessments for young person.

☐ _____

_____

☐ _____

_____

☐ _____

_____

27 www.childrensmentalhealthweek.org.uk
28 www.time-to-change.org.uk/get-involved/time-talk-day

What worked well, and what would you do differently?

Remember that self-care is an essential part of my daily routine.

- I am grateful for: _____

  _____

  _____

- My mental wellbeing action for this week is to ensure I _____

  _____

  _____

- What I am currently reading/listening to: _____

  _____

  _____

Summary for Week 1

1. This week is about 'landing safely' and planning for Children's Mental Health Week and Time to Talk Day in early February.

2. Delegate to staff and students the responsibility for running an activity or event so that the impact of this week will be felt.

3. January is a really important month to destigmatize the topic of mental health and ensure we set up structures later in the year promoting a culture where everyone is kind to others and kind to themselves.

Week 2

Purpose of the week: Plan gathering quantitative and/or qualitative data on the impact of the wellbeing zone and the impact the anti-bullying ambassadors and the anti-bullying room are having in the school on students.

My goals:

☐ Reflect on the results of the student wellbeing survey to check for impact. Are the provisions you have in place commensurate with students' needs? Listen to the student voices.

☐ Consult with the SLT on the results.

☐ Plan a strategy moving forward to ensure that what the school does offer is commensurate with student needs.

☐ Meet with the MHFA to discuss safeguarding issues, students at risk and strategies for support, overseeing interventions and establishing links with external agencies and professionals. Ensure the individual student support mental wellbeing plan is filled in and parents are contacted (see Appendix 5).

☐ _____

   _____

☐ _____

   _____

☐ _____

   _____

What worked well, and what would you do differently?

Remember that self-care is an essential part of my daily routine.

- I am grateful for: _____

  _____

  _____

- My mental wellbeing action for this week is to ensure I _____

  _____

  _____

- What I am currently reading/listening to: _____

  _____

  _____

Summary for Week 2

1. This week is about reflecting on the impact of the services your school has put in place. If we don't measure impact, we will never really know how effective the interventions have been.

2. If you still have to do it, then the purpose of the questionnaire is to find out how students feel about some aspects of their life at school – in particular, what things cause them to worry or become anxious, who they would turn to if they were worried, anxious or distressed, what type of support services they prefer and how they feel about their school environment, what they like about it and what they don't. Stress to students you have not asked for any personal details about them so their responses will be anonymous.

3. I found using Microsoft Forms very simple and user-friendly and it enabled me to just send the link to students. All the results were automatically collated for me to enable really easy reading using graphics.

Week 3

Purpose of the week: Prepping children's mental health well so that all stakeholders in the school feel invited and involved.

My goals:

☐ Delegate student and staff responsibilities for Children's Mental Health Week coming up. Have a meeting with staff and students, asking them to submit ideas.

☐ Ensure that each of the rooms in the wellbeing zone is running activities for students to take part. Ideas could be:

- Freedom 2B: inspirational LGBTQ+ people who have 'found their brave', 'come hear all about it'.

- Q (quiet space): #sloweating, quiet reading and the benefits of quiet and being still and reading.

- AB (anti-bullying space): role-plays, creating paper cut-out 'anti-bullying kind hands' where the palms and five fingers highlight a kind act towards another peer; Happy Bag handouts that are colourful paper gift bags with motivational, reflective and positive sayings where you are gifted a saying to lift your spirits and emphasize connectedness.

- YC (young carers space): screening of *Spiderman* or *Wonder Woman*. There is a shero or hero in every young carer.

- Wellbeing room: mindfulness, mindful colouring, gratitude journal.

☐ Build these activities into a #wellbeingsquare Bingo card where students who participate at lunchtimes in the rooms can collect house points.

☐ Meet with the SLT to discuss the week for staff and students, and approve activities and foci.

☐ Advertise in the staff room. Faculties host a Tea and Talk session as part of the Time To Talk Day. See the planner for next week with all the details.

☐ Meet with the MHFA to discuss safeguarding issues, students at risk and strategies for support, overseeing interventions and establishing links with external agencies and professionals. Ensure the individual student support mental wellbeing plan is filled in and parents are contacted (see Appendix 5).

☐ _____

☐ _____

☐ _____

What worked well, and what would you do differently?

Remember that self-care is an essential part of my daily routine.

- I am grateful for: _____

  _____

  _____

- My mental wellbeing action for this week is to ensure I _____

  _____

  _____

- What I am currently reading/listening to: _____

  _____

  _____

Summary for Week 3

1. This week is about ensuring that our dialogue is not only about mental health challenges and mental health illnesses, but also about what it takes to have positive mental health.

2. In working on Children's Mental Health Week it is advisable to ensure (a) as many stakeholders in the school – students, staff and governors – are involved to ensure maximum engagement; and (b) the focus is on what it takes to have positive mental health and to celebrate our strengths and the relationships we have, to find our inner drive and sense of gratitude, to ensure people are not overloaded and there is maximum engagement – the key here is to delegate and get the students to lead the activities in each space that is hosting a Children's Mental Health Week activity.

Week 4

Purpose of the week: To prepare all the activities for staff to take part in their faculties for the Time to Talk Day.

My goals:

☐ Send an email inviting heads of faculties to plan two lunchtimes together, one with their own faculty and another with another faculty where they will play some of the activities provided by the Time to Talk website.[29] I've tried to keep this just for staff as we also have a #childrensmentalhealthweek focus just for the students.

☐ Download the staff Work Activity Pack[30] and print off the resources so staff can choose which one they would like to use.

☐ Meet with the MHFA to discuss safeguarding issues, students at risk and strategies for support, overseeing interventions and establishing links with external agencies and professionals. Ensure the individual student support mental wellbeing plan is filled in and parents are contacted (see Appendix 5).

☐ _____

_____

☐ _____

_____

☐ _____

_____

29 www.time-to-change.org.uk/get-involved/time-talk-day
30 www.time-to-change.org.uk/sites/default/files/TtC%20Workplace%20Activity%20Pack%202020_0.
    pdf

What worked well, and what would you do differently?

Remember that self-care is an essential part of my daily routine.

- I am grateful for: _____

    _____

    _____

- My mental wellbeing action for this week is to ensure I _____

    _____

    _____

- What I am currently reading/listening to: _____

    _____

    _____

Summary for Week 4

1. Whilst it is Children's Mental Health Week in the first week of February, also be aware that it coincides with Time to Talk Day in that same week.

2. This day is all about destigmatizing mental health, having the conversation, and focusing on what it takes to have positive mental health. The DMHL can use the Time to Talk Day as a perfect opportunity for staff to develop an awareness of their own mental health and to get to know each other and perhaps start the conversation. The activities on the Time to Talk website are fabulous.

3. There is an Employer Action Plan,[31] which is a great way to start the conversation with your employer.

---

31 www.time-to-change.org.uk/get-involved/get-your-workplace-involved/employer-pledge/develop-your-action-plan

Week 5

Purpose of the week: To prepare students to talk about the concept of *love* for a Valentine's Day theme on 14 February.

My goals:

- ☐ This week is Children's Mental Health Week. Run all the activities planned. Ask students to hand in Bingo cards at the end so you can monitor the level of engagement (see Week 3 for ideas).

- ☐ This week will also see staff lunch sessions and Tea and Talk sessions taking place to mark Time to Talk Day. Ask staff to let you know their thoughts on taking the time to check on each other and suggestions for how we can keep this up for the whole year.

- ☐ To coincide with Valentine's Day, meet with the MHFA and wellbeing ambassadors to discuss the concept of self-compassion. Prepare an assembly on the concept of love and self-compassion and get the message out there that love and kindness start with applying them to yourself (see Appendix 1).

- ☐ Meet with the MHFA to discuss safeguarding issues, students at risk and strategies for support, overseeing interventions and establishing links with external agencies and professionals. Ensure the individual student support mental wellbeing plan is filled in and parents are contacted (see Appendix 5).

- ☐ _____

  _____

- ☐ _____

  _____

- ☐ _____

  _____

What worked well, and what would you do differently?

Remember that self-care is an essential part of my daily routine.

- I am grateful for: _____

  _____

  _____

- My mental wellbeing action for this week is to ensure I _____

  _____

  _____

- What I am currently reading/listening to: _____

  _____

  _____

Summary for Week 5

1. This week is about redefining the concept of love by getting the young people and teachers to think about the concept of self-compassion.

2. It might also be an idea to focus on what healthy relationships are in the mental health lessons this week, coinciding with Valentine's Day.

3. Staff lunch sessions and Tea and Talk sessions taking place to mark Time to Talk Day.

Week 6

Purpose of the week: Plan for Eating Disorders Awareness Week with the mental wellbeing ambassadors.

My goals:

☐ Meet with the wellbeing ambassadors to discuss what is a healthy body image, what is a negative body image and what is an eating disorder. Speak to the wellbeing ambassadors to discuss ideas for reaching out to the rest of the school.

☐ Raise awareness: create a podcast for parents and students and staff on what is a positive and negative body image and where to get support if you think someone has an eating disorder, or share podcasts and YouTube clips from other people.

☐ Set up links with local charities or experts or those in recovery to come and talk to the students about eating disorders, and ask for workshops or presentations to be made available for students.

☐ Review mental health and wellbeing curriculum delivery for after half term and check the sessions on healthy body image and eating disorders coincide with the campaign.

☐ Meet with the MHFA to discuss safeguarding issues, students at risk and strategies for support, overseeing interventions and establishing links with external agencies and professionals. Ensure the individual student support mental wellbeing plan is filled in and parents are contacted (see Appendix 5).

☐ _____

_____

☐ _____

_____

☐ _____

_____

What worked well, and what would you do differently?

Remember that self-care is an essential part of my daily routine.

- I am grateful for: _____

  _____

  _____

- My mental wellbeing action for this week is to ensure I _____

  _____

  _____

- What I am currently reading/listening to: _____

  _____

  _____

Summary for Week 6

1. This week is about tackling myths surrounding eating disorders and to start the conversation about what is a negative and what is a positive body image. Eating Disorders Awareness Week (EDAW)[32] generally takes place in the first week of March (straight after half term).

2. It is about ensuring young people understand and learn about the different types of eating disorders, what it feels like to have them, how they can help themselves and what help is out there for them.

3. If parents are concerned, you could also recommend books like *Eating Disorders: A Parent's Guide* and other helpful websites such as Body Gossip[33] and the Be Real Campaign.[34]

---

32 www.beateatingdisorders.org.uk
33 www.bodygossip.org
34 www.berealcampaign.co.uk

SPRING TERM 2B
Week 1

Purpose of the week: Eating Disorders Awareness Week and planning for Bipolar Day at the end of March.

My goals:

☐ Hold year group assemblies on body image. Encourage visiting speakers, who publicly share their stories and are verified case studies, to come and present assemblies so the students can connect with other people.

☐ Hold activities in your wellbeing zone for students to take part in at lunchtime, such as self-image and positivity exercises.

☐ Get students to write an article about this week and what has been learned for the school newsletter.

☐ Upload a podcast, video or weblinks onto the website for parents and students to access and listen to.

☐ Meet with the MHFA and wellbeing ambassadors to discuss Bipolar Day coming up at the end of March. Share key information about what bipolar means and why it's important to raise awareness about it.

☐ Meet with the MHFA to discuss safeguarding issues, students at risk and strategies for support, overseeing interventions and establishing links with external agencies and professionals. Ensure the individual mental health plan is filled in and parents are contacted (see Appendix 5).

☐ Together with the MHFA run intervention groups for young people with early signs of eating disorders linked to self-esteem and negative body image.

☐ _____

_____

☐ _____

_____

☐ _____

What worked well, and what would you do differently?

Remember that self-care is an essential part of my daily routine.

- I am grateful for: _____

  _____

  _____

- My mental wellbeing action for this week is to ensure I _____

  _____

  _____

- What I am currently reading/listening to: _____

  _____

  _____

Summary for Week 1

1. This week is about ensuring the school community explores body image, eating disorders and positivity about themselves and others, but is also able to unpick strategies for coping.

2. The Beat (Beat Eating Disorders) website[35] is very helpful as it provides information on all aspects of eating disorders.

3. You also need to find time this week to start prepping for Bipolar Day. Bipolar disorder is a serious mental illness that affects over a million people in the UK.[36]

---

35 www.beateatingdisorders.org.uk
36 See www.bipolaruk.org

Week 2

Purpose of the week: Plan for Stress Awareness Month.

My goals:

- ☐ Plan year group assemblies on stress awareness. Encourage visiting speakers, who publicly share their stories and are verified case studies, to come and present assemblies so the students can connect with other people.

- ☐ Plan activities in your wellbeing zone for students to take part in at lunch, such as mindfulness and stress busting exercises.

- ☐ Get students to write an article about managing exam stress for the school newsletter.

- ☐ Share podcasts or validated videos or record your own for parents and students to access and listen to.

- ☐ Meet with the MHFA and wellbeing ambassadors to discuss Stress Awareness Month coming up. Share key information about what stress is and why it's important to raise awareness about it.

- ☐ Meet with the MHFA to discuss safeguarding issues, students at risk and strategies for support, overseeing interventions and establishing links with external agencies and professionals. Ensure the individual student support mental wellbeing plan is filled in and parents are contacted (see Appendix 5).

- ☐ Together with the MHFA, plan to run intervention groups for young people with early signs of stress and anxiety.

- ☐ _____

  _____

- ☐ _____

  _____

- ☐ _____

  _____

What worked well, and what would you do differently?

Remember that self-care is an essential part of my daily routine.

- I am grateful for: _____

  _____

  _____

- My mental wellbeing action for this week is to ensure I _____

  _____

  _____

- What I am currently reading/listening to: _____

  _____

  _____

Summary for Week 2

1. This week is about planning for Stress Awareness Month. It has been held every April since 1992 to increase public awareness about both the causes and cures for our modern stress epidemic.[37] It is advisable to have one strategy for staff and one for students, such as eating healthily, taking breaks, exercise, staying connected and self-care.

2. It is important to build into the school's culture awareness of the signs of stress, of how workload can contribute to stress, and a sensitivity that we are all human beings with personal narratives so we need to be compassionate and empathetic, that we all need to take ownership for managing our stress.

3. When staff assert themselves and say no to doing something, it may be more a case of prioritizing their own wellbeing rather than being difficult. If a school has a listening culture, balance can be achieved for all.

---

37 www.stress.org.uk/national-stress-awareness-month-2019

Week 3

Purpose of the week: Staff wellbeing and workload reduction.

My goals:

☐ Deliver a mental health briefing on the value of self-care and #teacher5aday.[38] Remind staff of the role of the HR manager and Education Support.[39] If the school does not have an HR manager, make sure a member of the SLT is properly trained to take on this role and has the time to attend to supporting staff.

☐ Meet with the SWAGS and minute concerns that must be fed back to the SLT. Reboot a staff buddy system, plan a staff wellbeing event such as Bake Off or an after-school social, and encourage faculties to have at least one lunch together a week.

☐ Meet with the wellbeing ambassadors and discuss how they can lead a campaign of random acts of kindness towards teachers.

☐ Work with the head teacher to conduct a teacher workload survey using the Department for Education 'School workload reduction toolkit'.[40]

☐ Review the mental health and wellbeing curriculum delivery for after half term.

☐ Meet with the MHFA to discuss safeguarding issues, students at risk and strategies for support, overseeing interventions and establishing links with external agencies and professionals. Ensure the individual student support mental wellbeing plan is filled in and parents are contacted (see Appendix 5).

☐ _____

_____

☐ _____

_____

☐ _____

_____

---

38 Reah, M. (2019) '#teacher5aday: Why I started it, what we're doing now, and its impact.' SSAT, 1 November. Available at: www.ssatuk.co.uk/blog/teacher5aday-why-i-started-it-what-were-doing-now-and-its-impact

39 www.educationsupport.org.uk

40 www.gov.uk/guidance/school-workload-reduction-toolkit#identify-workload-issues-in-your-school

What worked well, and what would you do differently?

Remember that self-care is an essential part of my daily routine.

- I am grateful for: _____

_____

_____

- My mental wellbeing action for this week is to ensure I _____

_____

_____

- What I am currently reading/listening to: _____

_____

_____

Summary for Week 3

1. This week is about addressing staff workload. This is a recognized national issue, and if we are to improve the staff retention and recruitment crisis, engaging in this research will help you hear the different voices of your staff on issues regarding their mental wellbeing.

2. Work with the head teacher to conduct a teacher workload survey using the Department for Education 'School workload reduction toolkit'.[41]

3. Deliver a mental health briefing on the value of self-care and #teacher5aday. Remind staff of the role of the HR manager and Education Support.[42]

---

41 www.gov.uk/guidance/school-workload-reduction-toolkit
42 www.educationsupport.org.uk/?gclid=CjwKCAiAgJWABhArEiwAmNVTB6gyc46E7NEiEu5BRnegO3lyiVivQUCuh7o4fVWeImLrUAqTd74eZhoCorQQAvD_BwE

Week 4

Purpose of the week: Student wellbeing, Bipolar Day and mindfulness practice.

My goals:

- ☐ Deliver a briefing with staff on how to lead a 1-minute grounded breathing mindfulness exercise (part of the Mind Up programme[43]) at the start and end of their lessons (this may be a reminder session as you may already be using this in your school).

- ☐ Deliver assemblies with all year groups and remind students where they can go to talk to someone if they need support, teaching students how their brain responds to stress (the limbic system) and preparing them for creating a calm mindset for thoughtful decision-making, led by the prefrontal cortex. Teach the core practice, the 1-minute grounded breathing exercise (again, this may be a reminder session if you are already using this in your school).

- ☐ Run activities in the wellbeing zone with strategies for dealing with stress and anxiety, such as journal writing, origami, writing poetry, mindfulness colouring in, etc.

- ☐ Meet with the mental health and wellbeing ambassadors to take them through guided mindfulness and to get feedback on how things are going in your student wellbeing zone.

- ☐ Continue to work with the head teacher on the teacher workload survey using the Department for Education 'School workload reduction toolkit'.[44]

- ☐ Review the mental health and wellbeing curriculum delivery for next term.

- ☐ Meet with the MHFA to discuss safeguarding issues, students at risk and strategies for support, overseeing interventions and establishing links with external agencies and professionals. Ensure the individual student support mental wellbeing plan is filled in and parents are contacted (see Appendix 5).

- ☐ _____

- ☐ _____

- ☐ _____

---

43   https://mindup.org/brain-break-at-home
44   www.gov.uk/guidance/school-workload-reduction-toolkit

What worked well, and what would you do differently?

Remember that self-care is an essential part of my daily routine.

- I am grateful for: _____

  _____

  _____

- My mental wellbeing action for this week is to ensure I _____

  _____

  _____

- What I am currently reading/listening to: _____

  _____

  _____

Summary for Week 4

1. This week is about supporting student wellbeing as part of a whole-school focus.

2. We are nearing the end of term now and the seniors will be feeling the pressure of the up-and-coming summer exams next term, plus schools will be nearing completion of the term's summative assessments. This week it's important to boost student mental health and wellbeing with strategies for coping.

3. If you haven't already, introduce the 1-minute grounded breathing exercise. I strongly urge a whole-school approach to using mindfulness. Controlled, focused breathing is an exercise in mindful awareness. When practised regularly it allows children to have clarity, to be reflective, to release stress and to make rational decisions.

Week 5

Purpose of the week: To plan for Dying Matters Awareness Week and self-assess progress with your mental health award.

My goals:

☐ Evaluate progress on the mental health award you are going for. Update the accreditation board on your progress.

☐ Plan to mark Dying Matters Awareness Week[45] in May. It's a great opportunity to explore the topic of death, to talk about loss and to celebrate life. The idea is to create a safe space for students and staff to talk about death, dying or grief, and for everyone to develop a better understanding of how we can support each other.

☐ Review your mental health curriculum for next term.

☐ Meet with the MHFA to discuss safeguarding issues, students at risk and strategies for support, overseeing interventions and establishing links with external agencies and professionals. Ensure the individual student support mental wellbeing plan is filled in and parents are contacted (see Appendix 5).

☐ _____

_____

☐ _____

_____

☐ _____

_____

---

45 www.dyingmatters.org/AwarenessWeek

What worked well, and what would you do differently?

Remember that self-care is an essential part of my daily routine.

- I am grateful for: _____
  _____
  _____

- My mental wellbeing action for this week is to ensure I _____
  _____
  _____

- What I am currently reading/listening to: _____
  _____
  _____

Summary for Week 5

1. If you are doing a mental health award you should be methodically gathering evidence.

2. Planning for Dying Matters Awareness Week can help young people explore the importance of listening to those who want to talk about death and gain a better understanding of how we can all support each other. A range of topics can be explored, from traumatic or sudden death to stillbirth and miscarriages and the links of surviving someone who has died and its links with mental health. Some people generate discussions about illness, death and dying using the arts to break down barriers in a sensitive way; others link up with local hospice and specialist palliative care centres, encouraging awareness about what people can do to help someone who is dying or a family who is suffering. Others bring in local undertakers to talk about their role in death, and some people link up with local faith groups, mosques or churches to explore the role of religion in death.

3. Review your mental health curriculum for next term, checking that it links up with the up-and-coming National Awareness days.

Week 6

Purpose of the week: To ensure all safeguarding disclosures have been tracked and their impact assessed and there has been a complete self-assessment of your termly progress as you prepare for the Easter break and the final stretch.

My goals:

- ☐ Evaluate your termly planner and see what you still need to embed or embed further.

- ☐ Meet with the MHFA to look at all cases that have been referred and track the impact of interventions and outcomes. Ensure no safeguarding disclosures have been missed or have not been tracked.

- ☐ Meet the SWAGS and sum up three positives and three suggestions for reducing workload.

- ☐ Meet with the wellbeing ambassadors and get feedback on what they feel young people will benefit from next term.

- ☐ Review children who will be a safeguarding concern over Easter. Work closely with the DSL on setting up support structures for them when school is closed.

- ☐ Check who needs supervision before the half term in terms of staff, the MHFA and, of course, the DSL and DMHL (see Chapters 2 and 9).

- ☐ Prepare for Stress Awareness Month when you get back. Go over the activities you have planned.

- ☐ _____
  _____

- ☐ _____
  _____

- ☐ _____
  _____

What worked well, and what would you do differently?

Remember that self-care is an essential part of my daily routine.

- I am grateful for: _____

  _____

  _____

- My mental wellbeing action for this week is to ensure I _____

  _____

  _____

- What I am currently reading/listening to: _____

  _____

  _____

Summary for Week 6

1. This week is about self-assessment for your termly planner. See what you still need to work on and let this inform your planning for next term.

2. Have a double session where you sit with the MHFA and pastoral team to evaluate the impact of interventions on students and strategies for moving forward next term. Identify who is coming off the list for interventions, who is staying on and who needs referrals, and start the referrals (they take time to be processed). Ensure all safeguarding disclosures have been followed up before the close of school term and there are strategies in place for support and intervention.

3. Make sure you have prepared vulnerable students about the up-and-coming holidays. This can often be a difficult time for young people where there are considerable challenges at home, or they lose the structure of the school day and trusted adults. Arm the young people with a phone number they can call if they are worried or need to disclose anything, as well as strategies for coping with their worries and anxiety.

SUMMER TERM 3A
Week 1

Purpose of the week: To deliver Stress Awareness Month events and activities.

My goals:

☐ Get student-led assemblies on managing stress.

☐ Encourage staff to adopt cross-curricular exercises that touch on the theme of managing stress and anxiety.

☐ Run activities in the wellbeing zone at lunchtimes that raise awareness and teach practical strategies.

☐ Meet the mental health ambassadors in your weekly session and check in on their safeguarding. Check in on their strategies for coping with stress.

☐ Update the school website on Stress Awareness Month.

☐ Send out articles in the newsletter on strategies for dealing with stress.

☐ Share podcasts or validated videos or record your own on managing stress (these can be used for PSHE delivery and/or shared with the wider parent and school community).

☐ Meet with the MHFA to discuss safeguarding issues, students at risk and strategies for support, overseeing interventions and establishing links with external agencies and professionals. Ensure the individual student support mental wellbeing plan is filled in and parents are contacted (see Appendix 5). Review risk assessments for the young person.

☐ _____

  _____

☐ _____

  _____

☐ _____

  _____

What worked well, and what would you do differently?

Remember that self-care is an essential part of my daily routine.

- I am grateful for: _____

  _____

  _____

- My mental wellbeing action for this week is to ensure I _____

  _____

  _____

- What I am currently reading/listening to: _____

  _____

  _____

Summary for Week 1

1. This week is about profiling Stress Awareness Month, and it would be advisable to have one strategy for staff and one for students.

2. It is important to have clear strategies on supporting ourselves through stressful times, for example, eating healthily, taking breaks, exercise, staying connected and self-care.

Week 2

Purpose of the week: Train all staff on handling grief and coping with trauma.

My goals:

- ☐ Either deliver a twilight inset or inset CPD for staff on grief and coping with trauma.

- ☐ Share podcasts or validated videos or record your own, for young people on managing grief and bereavement, and share as part of the PSHE programme with students/ parents and the wider community.

- ☐ Meet the mental health ambassadors in your weekly session and check in on their safeguarding.

- ☐ Invite speakers in to share in assemblies on grief and bereavement and coping strategies.

- ☐ Run sessions at lunchtimes in the wellbeing zone, raising awareness on strategies to support grief and bereavement.

- ☐ Meet with the MHFA and review interventions for students experiencing grief and loss.

- ☐ Meet with the MHFA to discuss safeguarding issues, students at risk and strategies for support, overseeing interventions and establishing links with external agencies and professionals. Ensure the individual student support mental wellbeing plan is filled in and parents are contacted (see Appendix 5). Review risk assessments for the young person.

- ☐ _____

_____

- ☐ _____

_____

- ☐ _____

_____

What worked well, and what would you do differently?

Remember that self-care is an essential part of my daily routine.

- I am grateful for: _____

  _____

  _____

- My mental wellbeing action for this week is to ensure I _____

  _____

  _____

- What I am currently reading/listening to: _____

  _____

  _____

Summary for Week 2

1. This week is about understanding the impact of grief on a young person, ensuring they are feeling understood and heard, identifying strengths and that they are more than grief or loss, alleviating fears around letting go by letting in reframed experiences, feelings or thoughts at the same time as letting go of what we feel we need to and moving forward. It is also about exploring issues around acceptance, guilt, blame and validating feelings of overwhelm. Finally, it's important to explore hopes for the future, understanding the importance of experiencing other aspects of life aside from grief and loss. A useful website is Cruse Bereavement Care.[46]

2. Deliver CPD on grief and bereavement and ensure a lesson on grief and loss is explored in the mental health curriculum. This will link nicely into Dying Matters Awareness Week, which takes place in May.

3. Connect with people in your school and community who can share their journeys and encourage the young people to listen with empathy and understand the different strategies and support structures out there to help them and their families.

---

46 www.cruse.org.uk

Week 3

Purpose of the week: Planning ahead for national themed mental health awareness days.

My goals:

- ☐ Plan for Dying Matters Awareness Week, which takes place in May.

- ☐ Plan for Mental Health Awareness Week (hosted by the Mental Health Foundation).[47]

- ☐ Plan for Healthy Eating Awareness Week in June.

- ☐ Plan for Volunteers' Week, which is a chance to celebrate and say thank you for the fantastic contribution millions of volunteers make across the UK. It takes place 1–7 June every year, and is an opportunity to celebrate volunteering in all its diversity.[48]

- ☐ Meet the mental health ambassadors in your weekly session and check in on their safeguarding.

- ☐ Meet with the MHFA to discuss safeguarding issues, students at risk and strategies for support, overseeing interventions and establishing links with external agencies and professionals. Ensure the individual student support mental wellbeing plan is filled in and parents are contacted (see Appendix 5). Review risk assessments for the young person.

- ☐ _____
  _____

- ☐ _____
  _____

- ☐ _____
  _____

---

47 www.mentalhealth.org.uk/campaigns/mental-health-awareness-week
48 https://volunteersweek.org

What worked well, and what would you do differently?

Remember that self-care is an essential part of my daily routine.

- I am grateful for: _____
  _____

- My mental wellbeing action for this week is to ensure I _____
  _____

- What I am currently reading/listening to: _____
  _____

Summary for Week 3

1. This week is about planning for the national awareness days later this term or next term. As usual, have a conversation with the wellbeing ambassadors about what can be done in your wellbeing zone at lunchtimes; have conversations with your pastoral leads on what can be done in assemblies; build in lessons into the PSHE curriculum; and encourage all teachers to weave in cross-curricular themes into their lessons.

2. Dying Matters Awareness Week is a great opportunity to explore death, talk about loss and celebrate life. To be able to talk about death and dying starts with having conversations about it.

3. Mental Health Awareness Week is the UK's national week to raise awareness of mental health and mental health problems and to inspire action to promote the message of good mental health for all. The Mental Health Foundation has run it since 2001.

4. BNF Healthy Eating Week aims to bring people together for a dedicated week, focusing on key health messages and promoting healthy habits. Some of the health challenges are: eat more wholegrains; vary your veg; drink plenty; move more; be mind kind; get active together; and eat together.

5. Volunteers' Week is important to celebrate because of its very strong links with positive mental health and being part of a community. It is important we make our students aware of the benefits of becoming a volunteer and the diverse volunteering roles that are available. As well as helping others, volunteering has been shown to have a positive impact on the lives of those who volunteer, assisting volunteers in gaining new skills and boosting self-esteem.

Week 4

Purpose of the week: Looking ahead and booking ahead, reviewing and auditing, and marking Dying Matters Awareness Week.

My goals:

☐ Dying Matters Awareness Week is in May. You may have planned assemblies, speakers, mental health and wellbeing lessons to coincide with this theme. A great one would be to encourage the art, drama and dance subjects to mark it with cross-curricular work.

☐ Plan for Volunteers' Week in two weeks' time. You may want to connect with some local organizations where young people get to volunteer or the organizations volunteer in your school (see Summer Term 3b, Week 1).

☐ Start thinking about what you want to go into the SDP for the next academic year.

☐ Book in speakers for assemblies and inset days for next year (linked to the National Awareness days).

☐ Start to have the conversation with the SLT on training you would like staff to have (insets and CPD).

☐ Review and update your register and contact list of external agencies and providers of support services. Clarify contact, support offered, cost and estimated waiting list.

☐ Review delivery of the mental health curriculum for this term.

☐ Review the mental health curriculum for next half term.

☐ Meet the mental health ambassadors in your weekly session and check in on their safeguarding.

☐ Meet with the MHFA to discuss safeguarding issues, students at risk and strategies for support, overseeing interventions and establishing links with external agencies and professionals. Ensure the individual student support mental wellbeing plan is filled in and parents are contacted (see Appendix 5). Review risk assessments for the young person.

☐ _____

☐ _____

☐ _____

What worked well, and what would you do differently?

Remember that self-care is an essential part of my daily routine.

- I am grateful for: _____

  _____

  _____

- My mental wellbeing action for this week is to ensure I _____

  _____

  _____

- What I am currently reading/listening to: _____

  _____

  _____

Summary for Week 4

1. Mark Dying Matters Awareness Week with speakers, events and lessons. Raise awareness on your website and link up with your local hospice and palliative care centre.

2. This week is about planning. A key part to rolling out a whole-school strategy is not springing any surprises on the SLT and the academic and pastoral calendar. Get in early – look at your national awareness days and plan ahead. Book in assemblies, speakers and performances, trainers and training days.

3. Refer to your reviewed yearly planner and start planning your updated termly planner and then make bookings accordingly. I always start with staff CPD to support the mental wellbeing of our students and also ensure there is focus on staff wellbeing.

Week 5

Purpose of the week: Run activities for Mental Health Awareness Week.

My goals:

☐ Run activities in your wellbeing zone or #wellbeingsquare, for example:

- Freedom 2B room: impact of homophobia on mental health.

- Q room: strategies for being in the present, being still, reflective.

- AB room: the impact of bullying on mental health and why we should be upstanders and report any bullying in person or online; how to stay safe online.

- YC room: the impact of being a young carer and living with a parent or a sibling who has a mental health challenge and strategies for coping and people and places you can talk to.

- Wellbeing space: running mindfulness sessions, how to listen without judgement, what empathy looks like, websites and contacts available to students for support.

☐ Run activities with staff such as a staff buddy system in faculty areas, raise awareness of Education Support,[49] encourage line managers to have the first item on the agenda, 'How is your wellbeing?'

☐ Run a #teacher5aday campaign emphasizing the five key principles to support positive mental wellbeing.

☐ Meet the mental health ambassadors in your weekly session and check in on their safeguarding.

☐ Meet with the MHFA to discuss safeguarding issues, students at risk and strategies for support, overseeing interventions and establishing links with external agencies and professionals. Ensure the individual student support mental wellbeing plan is filled in and parents are contacted (see Appendix 5). Review risk assessments for the young person.

☐ _____

☐ _____

☐ _____

---

49 www.educationsupport.org.uk

What worked well, and what would you do differently?

Remember that self-care is an essential part of my daily routine.

- I am grateful for: _____

  _____

  _____

- My mental wellbeing action for this week is to ensure I _____

  _____

  _____

- What I am currently reading/listening to: _____

  _____

  _____

Summary for Week 5

1. This week is about profiling Mental Health Awareness Month. This not only helps young people realize how we all have mental health, but also raises awareness and encourages empathy and support to ensure no one feels they can't talk about it. Above all, it is about destigmatizing.

2. Ways in which you can raise community awareness during Mental Health Awareness Month:

   - Talk about it.

   - Share your experience.

   - Encourage empathy.

   - Educate yourself about mental illness.

   - Volunteer in your local community to help those who are struggling.

   - Be visible on social media.

3. Ensure the young people are leading in assemblies and activities, and encourage staff to come on board and to carry on the conversation in tutor periods and cross-curricular work.

SUMMER TERM 3B
Week 1

Purpose of the week: Run Volunteers' Week.

My goals:

☐ Have various charities come into school explaining how the students can volunteer and help their charities. Students can take away leaflets and get involved in tutor groups.

☐ Show a short film highlighting the contribution of Royal Voluntary Service (RVS) volunteers and NHS Volunteer Responders.[50]

☐ The school chooses a charity and students in each year group volunteer to get involved with certain activities, from fundraising to making donation boxes.

☐ Music and drama and dance students hold showcase events and perform for local groups to combat loneliness and isolation.

☐ Volunteer to help in the local residential care home, homeless centre, park and National Trust, recycle campaign, clean your beach, park, rivers, etc.

☐ Review delivery of the mental health curriculum for this term.

☐ Meet the mental health ambassadors in your weekly session and check in on their safeguarding.

☐ Prepare for the BNF Healthy Eating Week next week in the canteen. Meet with the canteen staff at least a week ahead to coordinate.

☐ Meet with the MHFA to discuss safeguarding issues, students at risk and strategies for support, overseeing interventions and establishing links with external agencies and professionals. Ensure the individual student support mental wellbeing plan is filled in and parents are contacted (see Appendix 5). Review risk assessments for the young person.

☐ _____

☐ _____

☐ _____

---

50 www.royalvoluntaryservice.org.uk/virtual-village-hall/activity/volunteers-week-tribute

What worked well, and what would you do differently?

Remember that self-care is an essential part of my daily routine.

- I am grateful for: _____

  _____

- My mental wellbeing action for this week is to ensure I _____

  _____

- What I am currently reading/listening to: _____

  _____

Summary for Week 1

1. This week is about raising awareness on Volunteers' Week.[51] Volunteers' Week is an opportunity to celebrate volunteering in all its diversity. As well as helping others and looking great on student CVs, there are three good reasons to promote this week in your school:

   - It raises mental wellbeing. By helping others you are not only benefiting their wellbeing, but also helping your own wellbeing and mental health too.

   - It encourages resilience. Volunteering often involves meeting new people and doing new things and being out of your comfort zone. Trying something new is an excellent way to keep learning and has a positive impact on our mental wellbeing.

   - It builds relationships between students and their local community. This is great for community cohesion and wellbeing, but can also be advantageous when students are looking for employment opportunities later on in their lives.

2. This week is about connecting with the local charities and community groups you are supporting and encouraging the young people to get involved with their local communities.

---

51 https://volunteersweek.org/about-volunteers-week/why-is-volunteering-important

Week 2

Purpose of the week: To run the BNF Healthy Eating Week focusing on key health messages and promoting healthy habits, from eating to exercise.

My goals:

☐ Advertise the BNF Healthy Eating Week in the canteen. Have a different theme each day promoting awareness, for example:

- Focus on wholegrains and their value in the Breakfast Club. Promote porridge or a wholegrain breakfast cereal such as bran flakes at breakfast time and wholegrain rye crackers with peanut butter as a snack.

- Promote 5 a day portions of vegetables and fruit and encourage different colours to be tried as different-coloured fruit and vegetables.

- Provide different amounts and types of vitamins and minerals.

- Promote the importance of water and drinking 6–8 glasses a day. Encourage young people to stay hydrated and to have a drink with meals, keeping a reusable water bottle in their bag to sip from all day.

- Promote exercise and being active for at least 30 minutes every day (ranging from moderate to vigorous intensity).

☐ Run fitness and exercise classes before school, lunchtime and after school. Invite the local fitness instructor to hold fun classes, from hula hooping to Hatha yoga.

☐ Meet the mental health ambassadors in your weekly session and check in on their safeguarding.

☐ Meet with the MHFA to discuss safeguarding issues, students at risk and strategies for support, overseeing interventions and establishing links with external agencies and professionals. Ensure the individual student support mental wellbeing plan is filled in and parents are contacted (see Appendix 5). Review risk assessments for the young person.

☐ _____

  _____

☐ _____

  _____

☐ _____

  _____

What worked well, and what would you do differently?

Remember that self-care is an essential part of my daily routine.

- I am grateful for: _____

  _____

  _____

- My mental wellbeing action for this week is to ensure I

  _____

  _____

- What I am currently reading/listening to: _____

  _____

  _____

Summary for Week 2

1. This week is about the BNF Healthy Eating Week and is all about raising awareness for the charity and how to eat more healthily, and thanks to this, to live a better life! It is hosted by the British Nutrition Foundation (BNF).[52]

2. Its aim is to bring the UK together for a dedicated week focusing on key health messages and promoting healthy habits. An example of the health challenges you could run in your school are:

   Eat more wholegrains (Monday); vary your veg (Tuesday); drink plenty (Wednesday); move more (Thursday); be mind kind (Friday); get active together (Saturday); eat together (Sunday).

3. The BNF has some fabulous resources providing challenges and marketing material to raise awareness in schools and in classrooms.[53]

---

52 For guidance on how schools can get involved, see www.nutrition.org.uk/healthyliving/hew/bnfhew20. html

53 www.nutrition.org.uk/healthyliving/hew/bnfhew20.html

Week 3

Purpose of the week: Review your whole-school mental health and wellbeing strategy and ensure mental health is in the forthcoming year SDP (school development plan).

My goals:

☐ Plan dates with the SLT to continue mental health early morning briefings – 10-minute slots to raise awareness and key concepts and strategies.

☐ Meet with the SLT and build in a whole-school culture of mental health and wellbeing into the forthcoming year SDP. Focus on:

- Leadership and strategy.

- Staff support and wellbeing.

- Student support and wellbeing.

- Staff professional development and learning about mental health.

- Working with parents and carers.

- Working with external services.

☐ Based on how you have RAGed yourself (red, amber or green[54]) with your termly focus this year (see Chapter 12), build in objectives that have yet to be fully embedded.

☐ Meet the mental health ambassadors in your weekly session and check in on their safeguarding.

☐ Meet with the MHFA to discuss safeguarding issues, students at risk and strategies for support, overseeing interventions and establishing links with external agencies and professionals. Ensure the individual student support mental wellbeing plan is filled in and parents are contacted (see Appendix 5). Review risk assessments for the young person.

☐ _____

☐ _____

☐ _____

---

54 Red amber green reporting is essentially a traffic light system that tells you that red statuses are incomplete or still need to be addressed, amber signals some progress has been made but more needs to be done and green means that everything is on track and on the way to being embedded.

What worked well, and what would you do differently?

Remember that self-care is an essential part of my daily routine.

- I am grateful for: _____

  _____

- My mental wellbeing action for this week is to ensure I _____

  _____

- What I am currently reading/listening to: _____

  _____

Summary for Week 3

1. This week is about making sure the impact of the school's mental health and wellbeing initiatives are being measured, that you are feeding back the results to the SLT and then planning a strategic focus for the following year. If it is not in the SDP, you will struggle to get things actioned. However, if it is in the SDP, it becomes a mandate for all staff. It is part of the school's strategic vision and therefore it is everyone's responsibility to help work towards embedding it.

2. We need to be reminded of the words from the Department for Education's *Mental Health and Behaviour in Schools*[55] that the culture, ethos and environment of the school can have a profound influence on both pupil and staff mental wellbeing. Environments that are hostile, aggressive, chaotic or unpredictable can be harmful to mental health, and can lead to stressful teaching and working conditions.

3. The way to be an effective DMHL is to be strategic in your focus and to work alongside other key foci the school's strategic team want to develop. The mental health and wellbeing initiatives for staff and students are part of the wider culture, ethos and learning and working environment, and along with a focus on teaching and learning, behaviour, curriculum and tracking and assessments, the DMHL should see how you can advise, collaborate and feed into the initiatives and not be seen as a stand-alone concept.

---

55 Department for Education (2018) *Mental Health and Behaviour in Schools*. Available at: https://assets. publishing.service.gov.uk/government/uploads/system/uploads/attachment_data/file/755135/Mental_ health_and_behaviour_in_schools__.pdf

Week 4

Purpose of the week: Prepare vulnerable students for the holidays, and review.

My goals:

☐ Deliver a short, early morning mental health briefing for staff on the role they can play in preparing vulnerable students in their tutor groups or classes for the holidays. All students will have at least one teacher they connect with. Take staff through the various stages of: *listen, connect with people, connect online, routine planning, wellbeing toolbox creating* and *writing an action plan.*

☐ Meet the SWAGS. Review what has been achieved, what is still to be achieved and build it into the SDP. Write into the school diary or planner SWAG meetings for the following year, as part of directed time.

☐ Review plans for inset days and training you are going to deliver in the new academic year.

☐ Review the mental health curriculum and delivery for next year.

☐ Review the school website presence of mental health support for parents and support and podcasts and videos available for your school community.

☐ If you are participating in a mental health award or kite Mark program - audit and, review what you have achieved and where you are up to, and set a date for assessment.

☐ Meet the mental health ambassadors in your weekly session and check in on their safeguarding and preparing for the holidays.

☐ Meet with the MHFA to discuss safeguarding issues, students at risk and strategies for support, overseeing interventions and establishing links with external agencies and professionals.

☐ _____

_____

☐ _____

_____

☐ _____

_____

What worked well, and what would you do differently?

Remember that self-care is an essential part of my daily routine.

- I am grateful for: _____

  _____

- My mental wellbeing action for this week is to ensure I _____

  _____

- What I am currently reading/listening to: _____

  _____

Summary for Week 4

1. This week is about preparing vulnerable students, particularly those with mental health difficulties, for how to prepare for the long school holidays.

2. Dr Pooky Knightsmith coherently sums up what is needed.[56] Here are the key points:

   - Listen.

   - Help identify people who are there to support them (family, friends).

   - Offer support online, including useful websites and phone numbers they can email or call to talk to someone.

   - Plan a strict routine, including planning healthy meals and exercise.

   - Create their wellbeing toolbox that might include photos of people they care about, favourite books, reminders to listen to a favourite playlist, walking the dog or watching something funny, a letter from themselves or someone else, scented candles, an adult colouring book, etc.

   - Write an action plan. This could be a visual daily plan that splits the day into clear manageable sections or set daily achievable aims with the objective of trying to achieve a minimum number each day.

56 Knightsmith, P. (2017) 'How to help vulnerable pupils prepare for the summer holidays.' SecEd, 7 June. Available at: www.sec-ed.co.uk/best-practice/how-to-help-vulnerable-pupils-prepare-for-the-summer-holidays

Week 5

Purpose of the week: To wrap up and plan for first week back in September.

My goals:

- ☐ Write into the school diary or planner as part of directed time SWAG meetings for the following year.

- ☐ Let staff know about Education Support,[57] the phone line charity, and its number, and what they can do to support staff over the holidays. Encourage staff to really switch off and practise #teacher5aday.

- ☐ Make plans for the staff wellbeing room as to how it can be better used next year.

- ☐ Get feedback from staff who were on rota in the student wellbeing zone, with suggestions for moving forward.

- ☐ Review the inset days and training you are going to deliver in the new academic year (see Appendix 1).

- ☐ Finalize the mental health curriculum and delivery for next year. Ensure ease of access by the relevant teachers.

- ☐ Update the school website presence of mental health support for parents as well as podcasts and videos available for your school community. Check their relevance and if the links work.

- ☐ Meet the mental health ambassadors in your weekly session and check in on their safeguarding and preparing for the holidays.

- ☐ Meet with the MHFA to discuss safeguarding issues, students at risk and strategies for support.

- ☐ Review children who will be a safeguarding concern over the summer holidays. Work closely with the DSL on setting up support structures for them when the school is closed.

- ☐ Check who needs supervision before the end of the school year in terms of staff, MHFA and, of course, the DSL and DMHL (see Chapters 2 and 9).

- ☐ _____

- ☐ _____

- ☐ _____

---

57 www.educationsupport.org.uk

What worked well, and what would you do differently?

Remember that self-care is an essential part of my daily routine.

- I am grateful for: _____

  _____

  _____

- My mental wellbeing action for this week is to ensure I _____

  _____

  _____

- What I am currently reading/listening to: _____

  _____

  _____

Summary for Week 5

1. Reflect on what could be better and listen to key staff and students. Adjust your focus and set it into the SDP. Plan for implementation the next academic year.

2. Ensure all referrals have been tracked, measured against outcomes and triaged for next steps, keeping parents informed. Check filing and access to information. Review children who will be a safeguarding concern over the summer holidays. Work with parents and carers and help the young people plan and prepare for the holidays, ensuring measures are in place for them to communicate any concerns they have.

3. Ensure supervision has been offered and key staff are able to go on holiday having received this support for their own emotional wellbeing.

Conclusion

No one doubts the importance of numeracy and literacy for the fast-changing world that lies ahead of young people, but if students are not emotionally literate about their own mental wellbeing, given targeted specific support with mental wellbeing challenges and in-depth exploration about what is a positive and what is a negative relationship and how to conduct themselves in real time and digital time, taught strategies for dealing with anxiety and stress and how to recognize that eating disorders and substance misuse are all forms of self-harm...then we are failing them. We will be churning out a shell that has been spoon-fed to enable them to pass an exam. But what about passing the resilience test called life? We need to change the narrative from only focusing on mental health illnesses and instead focus in our core curriculum on what it means and takes to be a 'well being'. In *Wise Up to Wellbeing in Schools*, the chief executive, Sarah Brennan, said:

> Students need education to include how to understand and look after their mental wellbeing – just like we learn how to look after our physical health. By shifting the focus to preventing mental wellbeing problems and building resilience we can do so much to improve the lives of so many. Good wellbeing on leaving school has a much greater impact on life outcomes than exam success.[1]

Our youth are having to be more 'grown up' than ever before. They are being presented with scenarios online that they are often not emotionally fully prepared for but are expected to make discerning choices about how to engage or not.

They are also witnessing adults working longer hours, showing clear signs of stress and often shocking examples of work–life balance. There are some alarming statistics from the Young Minds website.[2] Time spent with the family communicating is now only achieved through a concerted disciplined effort from everyone: to 'down tool' digital devices and to connect with each other.

In addition, Hannah Wilson, Founder of Diverse Educators, warns us that a significant risk factor for a mental health problem manifesting is the experience of race, religion or sexuality. She states: 'Anyone experiencing a mental health

---

1 Young Minds (no date) *Wise Up to Wellbeing in Schools*. Available at: https://youngminds.org.uk/media/1428/wise-up-prioritising-wellbeing-in-schools.pdf
2 Young Minds (no date) *Mental Health Statistics*. Available at: https://youngminds.org.uk/about-us/media-centre/mental-health-stats

problem should get both support and respect. However, for many people from Black, Asian and Minority Ethnic (BAME) communities this is still not the case. The reasons for this are complex but include systemic racism and discrimination as well as social and economic inequalities and mental health stigma.' Hannah Wilson and Diverse Educators are raising a key point that we need to take an intersectional approach to understanding mental health and self identity.

Looking forward, schools should be committed to diversity, equity and inclusion, at the same time as being committed to mental health and wellbeing – both should underpin the school's vision and practices from curriculum to staffing and policies.

Finally, there is staff wellbeing, often the Achilles heel of a school. In Amy Sayer's book, *Supporting Staff Mental Health in Your School,* she cites the following statistics that really hammer home why staff wellbeing has to be top of the agenda for any SDP:

- The UK Government's Health and Safety Executive[3] report from 2018 highlighted the fact that teaching has higher rates of reported work-related stress, depression or anxiety compared to other occupational groups (2100 reported cases per 100,000 for educational professionals, and only 1320 cases for other professions).

- Education Support,[4] the free online and phone support charity for educators, reported an increase in people contacting them by 28 per cent during 2017–19. The most alarming statistic is that between April 2018 and March 2019, the number of callers assessed as suicidal had increased by 57 per cent on the last year.[5]

- According to Education Support's Teacher Wellbeing Index 2018,[6] 76 per cent of teaching professionals have experienced behavioural, psychological or physical symptoms of stress compared to 60 per cent of all employees nationally.

The role of the DMHL is to oversee the culture of wellbeing throughout the school so all stakeholders, students, teachers and parents are made aware of what mental health is and how each individual can seek support or make changes in their lives. It is about overseeing all the initiatives, training, the tracking of the interventions and, of course, measuring impact and allowing the data to inform the future action

3   HSE (Health and Safety Executive) (2018) 'Health and safety statistics.' Available at: www.hse.gov.uk/statistics
4   www.educationsupport.org.uk
5   Education Support (2019) *Teacher Wellbeing Index 2019*. Available at: www.educationsupport.org.uk/sites/default/files/teacher_wellbeing_index_2019.pdf
6   Education Support (2018) *Teacher Wellbeing Index 2018*. Available at: www.educationsupport.org.uk/resources/research-reports/teacher-wellbeing-index-2018

plans needed to take the school closer towards adopting a whole-school approach. The DMHL might have to have some difficult conversations with representatives from governors to the SLT to ensure structural changes are made, ensuring life–work balance and early intervention is possible.

I hope this planner will help all DMHLs get started, or for those who are some way down the road, it can be a good reference tool to check what they might have missed or as a guide on how they can improve this leadership role ensuring they are at the epicentre of how the school develops its culture of mental wellbeing.

National Awareness Days

February

Time to Talk Day:[1] The aim is to get as many people as possible across England talking about mental wellbeing. By joining together on one day, we can break the silence that often surrounds mental wellbeing, and show that talking about this once-taboo issue doesn't need to be difficult.

Children's Mental Health Week:[2] This hopes to raise awareness of the benefits of getting children support at the earliest possible opportunity, and to encourage parents to talk openly with children about their feelings and getting help. Find out more about this week on the Place2Be website.[3]

March

Eating Disorders Awareness Week:[4] This is an international awareness event, fighting the myths and misunderstandings that surround eating disorders.

World Bipolar Day, 30 March:[5] The purpose of this day is to raise awareness of bipolar disorders and to improve sensitivity towards the illness. It is promoted by the International Bipolar Foundation and partners.

April

Stress Awareness Month:[6] During this annual 30-day period, healthcare professionals and health promotion experts join forces to increase public awareness about both the causes and cures for stress.

---

1   www.time-to-change.org.uk/get-involved/time-talk-day
2   www.childrensmentalhealthweek.org.uk
3   www.place2be.org.uk
4   www.b-eat.co.uk/support-us/eating-disorder-awareness-week
5   www.ibpf.org/blog/world-bipolar-day
6   http://stressawarenessmonth.com

May

Mental Health Awareness Week:[7] Raising awareness of mental wellbeing and wellbeing every year, promoted by the Mental Health Foundation.

Dying Matters Awareness Week:[8] This is an opportunity to place the importance of talking about dying, death and bereavement firmly on the national agenda. It takes place in early May.

June

Volunteers' Week, 1–7 June:[9] This is an annual event run by the National Council for Voluntary Organizations to celebrate volunteers and volunteering.

September

World Suicide Prevention Day, 10 September:[10] Organized by the International Association for Suicide Prevention and the World Health Organization, the purpose of the day is to promote worldwide commitment and action to prevent suicides.

October

World Mental Health Day, 10 October:[11] This has the overall objective of raising awareness of mental wellbeing issues around the world and mobilizing efforts in support of mental wellbeing. The day provides an opportunity for all stakeholders working on mental wellbeing issues to talk about their work, and what more needs to be done to make mental wellbeing care a reality for people worldwide. You can download a pack with ideas and resources for the day.

November

International Stress Awareness Week:[12] This is normally held in the first week of November each year, promoted by the International Stress Management Association (ISMA UK). Its purpose is to raise awareness of the effects of psychological distress in the workplace and of the many coping strategies and sources of help available to address it.

Anti-Bullying Week:[13] This is held during a week in the middle of November and is often accompanied by a theme.

---

7   www.mentalhealth.org.uk/campaigns/mental-health-awareness-week
8   www.dyingmatters.org/AwarenessWeek
9   https://volunteersweek.org/about-volunteers-week
10   www.iasp.info/wspd2020
11   www.mentalhealth.org.uk/campaigns/world-mental-health-day
12   https://isma.org.uk/isma-international-stress-awareness-week
13   See www.anti-bullyingalliance.org.uk and https://diana-award.org.uk

Recommended Reading List

ADHD (Attention Deficit Hyperactivity Disorder)

Steer, J. and Horstmann, K. (2009) *Helping Kids and Teens with ADHD in School: A Workbook for Classroom Support and Managing Transitions*. London: Jessica Kingsley Publishers.

Anxiety

Fitzpatrick, C. (2015) *A Short Introduction to Helping Young People Manage Anxiety*. London: Jessica Kingsley Publishers.

Lohmann, R.C. (2015) *Teen Anxiety: A CBT and ACT Activity Resource Book for Helping Anxious Adolescents*. London: Jessica Kingsley Publishers.

ASD (Autism Spectrum Disorder)

Cobbe, S. (2019) *Simple Autism Strategies for Home and School: Practical Tips, Resources and Poetry*. London: Jessica Kingsley Publishers.

Lawrence, C. (ed.) (2019) *Teacher Education and Autism: A Research-Based Practical Handbook*. London: Jessica Kingsley Publishers.

Murin, M., Hellriegel, J. and Mandy, W. (2016) *Autism Spectrum Disorder and the Transition into Secondary School: A Handbook for Implementing Strategies in the Mainstream School Setting*. London: Jessica Kingsley Publishers.

Wood, R. (2019) *Inclusive Education for Autistic Children: Helping Children and Young People to Learn and Flourish in the Classroom*. London: Jessica Kingsley Publishers.

Being able to talk about emotions

Azri, S. (2013) *Healthy Mindsets for Super Kids: A Resilience Programme for Children Aged 7–14*. London: Jessica Kingsley Publishers.

MacConville, R. and Rae, T. (2012) *Building Happiness, Resilience and Motivation in Adolescents: A Positive Psychology Curriculum for Well-Being*. London: Jessica Kingsley Publishers.

Seiler, L. (2008) *Cool Connections with CBT for Groups: Encouraging Self-Esteem, Resilience and Wellbeing in Children and Teens Using CBT Approaches* (2nd edn). London: Jessica Kingsley Publishers.

Body image

Macdonald, I. (2019) *Teen Substance Use, Mental Health and Body Image: Practical Strategies for Support*. London: Jessica Kingsley Publishers.

Bullying

Anti-Bullying Alliance (no date) *Bullying and Mental Health: Guidance for Teachers and Other Professionals*. Available at: www.anti-bullyingalliance.org.uk/sites/default/files/field/attachment/Mental-health-and-bullying-module-FINAL.pdf

Brown, K. (2018) *Bullying: A Review of the Evidence*. London: Education Policy Institute. Available at: https://epi.org.uk/publications-and-research/bullying-a-review-of-the-evidence

Department for Education (2014) *Mental Health and Behaviour in Schools*. [Updated 2018.] Available at: www.gov.uk/government/publications/mental-health-and-behaviour-in-schools--2

Gov.uk (no date) 'Bullying at school.' Available at: www.gov.uk/bullying-at-school

Katz, A. (2012) *Cyberbullying and E-safety: What Educators and Other Professionals Need to Know*. London: Jessica Kingsley Publishers.

Nassem, E. (2019) *A Teacher's Guide to Resolving School Bullying: Evidence-Based Strategies and Pupil-Led Interventions*. London: Jessica Kingsley Publishers.

Coming out and LGBTQ

Barnes, E. and Carlile, A. (2018) *How to Transform Your School into an LGBT+ Friendly Place: A Practical Guide for Nursery, Primary and Secondary Teachers*. London: Jessica Kingsley Publishers.

Charlesworth, J. (2020) *How to Stop Homophobic and Biphobic Bullying: A Practical Whole-School Approach*. London: Jessica Kingsley Publishers.

Counselling and creative therapies

D'Amico, D. (2016) *101 Mindful Arts-Based Activities to Get Children and Adolescents Talking: Working with Severe Trauma, Abuse and Neglect Using Found and Everyday Objects*. London: Jessica Kingsley Publishers.

Drabble, C. (2019) *Introducing a School Dog: Our Adventures with Doodles the Schnoodle*. London: Jessica Kingsley Publishers.

Knightsmith, P. (2016) *The Healthy Coping Colouring Book and Journal: Creative Activities to Help Manage Stress, Anxiety and Other Big Feelings*. London: Jessica Kingsley Publishers.

Lozier, C. (2018) *DBT Therapeutic Activity Ideas for Working with Teens: Skills and Exercises for Working with Clients with Borderline Personality Disorder, Depression, Anxiety, and Other Emotional Sensitivities*. London: Jessica Kingsley Publishers.

Luxmoore, N. (2006) *Working with Anger and Young People*. London: Jessica Kingsley Publishers.

Tait, A. and Dunn, B. (2018) *Conversation Starters for Direct Work with Children and Young People: Guidance and Activities for Talking About Difficult Subjects*. London: Jessica Kingsley Publishers.

Having a mental health conversation with a child

Luxmoore, N. (2014) *Essential Listening Skills for Busy School Staff: What to Say When You Don't Know What to Say*. London: Jessica Kingsley Publishers.

Loneliness

Stern, J. (2017) *Can I Tell You About Loneliness? A Guide for Friends, Family and Professionals*. London: Jessica Kingsley Publishers.

Mindfulness and calm
North, J. (2013) *Mindful Therapeutic Care for Children: A Guide to Reflective Practice*. London: Jessica Kingsley Publishers.

Obsessive-Compulsive Disorder (OCD)
Lewin, A.B. and Storch, E.A. (2017) *Understanding OCD: A Guide for Parents and Professionals*. London: Jessica Kingsley Publishers.

Panic attacks and exam stress
Steer, J. (2019) *Supporting Kids and Teens with Exam Stress in School: A Workbook*. London: Jessica Kingsley Publishers.

Self-compassion
Gumbrell, D. (2019) *LIFT! Going Up if Teaching Gets You Down*. St Albans: Critical Publishing Ltd.
Webb, S. (2018) *Can I Tell You About Compassion? A Helpful Introduction for Everyone*. London: Jessica Kingsley Publishers.

Self-esteem
Plummer, D. (2004) *Helping Adolescents and Adults to Build Self-Esteem: A Photocopiable Resource Book*. London: Jessica Kingsley Publishers.

Supporting staff mental health and wellbeing
Lovewell, K. (2012) *Every Teacher Matters: Inspiring Well-Being through Mindfulness*. St Albans: Ecademy Press.
Sayer, A. (2020) *Supporting Staff Mental Health in Your School*. London: Jessica Kingsley Publishers.

Trust and grief
Helton, S. (2017) *A Special Kind of Grief: The Complete Guide for Supporting Bereavement and Loss in Special Schools (and Other SEND Settings)*. London: Jessica Kingsley Publishers.
Holland, J. (2016) *Responding to Loss and Bereavement in Schools: A Training Resource to Assess, Evaluate and Improve the School Response*. London: Jessica Kingsley Publishers.

Whole-school wellbeing
Erasmus, C. (2019) *The Mental Health and Wellbeing Handbook for Schools: Transforming Mental Health Support on a Budget*. London: Jessica Kingsley Publishers.
Hulme, J. (2016) *The School of Wellbeing: 12 Extraordinary Projects Promoting Children and Young People's Mental Health and Happiness*. London: Jessica Kingsley Publishers.
Knightsmith, P. (2019) *The Mentally Healthy Schools Workbook: Practical Tips, Ideas and Whole-School Strategies for Making Meaningful Change*. London: Jessica Kingsley Publishers.

Young carers
Aldridge, J. (2018) *Can I Tell You About Being a Young Carer? A Guide for Friends, Family and Professionals*. London: Jessica Kingsley Publishers.

Other resources
Here are helpful phone numbers supported by charities to issue students and staff.

Ask Sam, Childline: Children can write a letter to Sam if there is something on their mind or they need support. They can also contact a counsellor for free or call 0800 1111.

Education Support: Need someone to talk to? Call the national helpline for education staff on 08000 562 561 – they offer free, confidential advice, 24/7.

Shout 85258: If a child is unable to cope and needs immediate support, they can text 'Shout' to 85258. It's free and available 24/7.

Staff Training: Awareness Raising, Teaching about Mental Health and Interventions

Our role as educators is not to diagnose or to replace CAMHS, but if we are to be proactive and pre-emptive with the language we use and the emotional literacy we teach in our curriculum and extra curriculum and the support structures we put in place, we could help prevent a situation from escalating.

A culture of mental wellbeing needs to be established for all stakeholders, and the training for all staff needs to be part of the whole-school development plan. This will, in turn, mean the mental health training is given the gravitas it deserves and relevance. It is the role of the DMHL to implement effective mental health training that ensures knowledge for staff of how to provide immediate support for students in need.

The first thing we need to assert is:

Mental health is everyone's responsibility - the mental health of every student is every staff member's responsibility. *Every staff member who has any contact with young people needs this training.*

I see it as part of the whole-school development plan, which needs to be broken down into different training sections that can be delivered over the course of one full 6-hour inset day, or preferably delivered over the course of an academic school year, building in the respective inset training days:

- Part 1: When to worry? The signs. Whose responsibility?

- Part 2: Having that first conversation. Listening model. Safeguarding (training staff and student wellbeing ambassadors).

- Part 3: Referral procedures. Self-referral and staff referral. How it works. Tracking and accessing the data.

- Part 4: Training in day-to-day strategies and ideas for one-to-one intervention.

- Part 5: Delivering effective mental health lessons in the curriculum and ensuring the environment is safe.

Part 1: Training in when to worry and whose responsibility it is

The key focus here is:

- The mental health of every student is everyone's responsibility.

- Question what *impact* this is having. Clarify with staff when to worry and how to spot the signs (change in diet, complaints of abdominal pains, nausea, self-esteem, appearance, personality change, withdrawn).

- Look for signs of longevity – how long has this been going on for?

- Remind staff about the school's safeguarding policy and the procedures to follow to file a report.

Part 2: Training in having the first conversation

- This training is about helping staff understand the role of confidentiality vs. safeguarding and knowing the safeguarding agreement you have to say quite near the point of the student opening up.

- This looks at what positive body language is; making the students feel like they have your full attention; learning to listen without judgement and not interrupting; reminding staff not to take over the narrative – this is not your story, it is theirs; and learning to sit with the silence if you have to.

- In this training session you should go through a listening model explained as follows.

Stage 1: Boundary issues

Go through the confidentiality and safeguarding terms with them:

Thank you for feeling safe enough that you want to come in and talk. I would like to reassure you that what you tell me will remain confidential. This means that I will not talk to anyone outside of this room about what you tell me.

Any discussion with the MHFA support worker or staff will not include your name, unless there is a need to break confidentiality.

I will not break confidence, unless you mention any of the following:

Physical, sexual or emotional abuse; threatened suicide; drug misuse that may be life threatening; possession or use of drugs on the school premises; pregnancy under the age of 16.

You also need to time limit the session (5 minutes/20 minutes).

Find out what they want to talk about. What are they expecting?

Stage 2: Listen

Accept, don't judge; use open body language; listen with empathy; paraphrase what they have told you; reflect; use open-ended questioning (who, what, how, when); and summarize.

Stage 3: Action – ask them what happens next

Who can they go to?

What are they able to do to help the situation?

When they have had problems in the past, how have they dealt with them?

Try not to say to them, 'Don't do this…' Ask for a response on possible ways forward instead.

Stage 4: Summary

What still needs to be solved?

What haven't they been able to do?

Ways forward: give them confidence, a message that they can do it.

Part 3: Training in a school's referral procedures

So, how can we best offer that support in a way that empowers the young person whilst ensuring that they get the help they need?

In my experience it is good to have two levels of support available and train your staff accordingly in how to make the best use of both:

- Self-referral, which encourages resilience and the students to help themselves.

- Teacher referral.

So what do self-referral spaces look like?

Self-referral spaces form part of what could be a wellbeing zone and could be made up of five discreet wellbeing areas. These spaces provide pre-emptive and proactive services to support students in their school setting, where they have some control over what happens, a place where for a few moments they can press 'pause' and gather their thoughts and emotions, a place where they feel less threatened or overwhelmed, and a place where they can talk to someone without fear of being judged.

With the clever use of existing spaces, teaching classrooms have become wellbeing spaces during school break periods (no expensive décor change needed, just effective signposting). With rooms open five days a week, each space is occupied by peer mentors and/or staff specially trained to deal with conversations and disclosures concerning mild to moderate mental health problems.

These 'pop-up' spaces are divided into five functional areas (the range of which will be dependent on each school's individual needs):

- Freedom 2B space, which focuses on encouraging discussions about difference and diversity.

- Q space for quiet personal reflection – something like the 'quiet carriage' on a train: so no talking!

- Anti-bullying space to communicate about relationship breakdowns, especially when the relationships become unhealthy.

- Young carers (YC) space, which is to recognize the role and existence of young carers and provide a place for them to connect with each other and a space for speakers to come and offer support.

- Wellbeing space, where young people can talk about matters that concern them.

These provide different spaces for different 'problems' but with the ultimate aim of de-escalating and providing early support. Mental health problems need to be destigmatized in the same way as special educational needs (SEN) support, and it is important to note that these pop-up spaces are seen as something separate from 'SEN space', otherwise many of the young people who are facing challenges won't visit as they don't see themselves as having a learning need.

These rooms need to be consistently open – every lunchtime – and with a trained staff member and peers in the rooms ready to listen and support.

Ideas for developing different rooms in your wellbeing zone:

- Freedom 2B space: hold weekly themed chats about being gay/having a family member who is gay/coming out/challenging homophobia in school. Invite a drama production to come and perform to students. Link up with Youth Stonewall[1] for visits and talks.

- YC space: send personalized invites to each of your listed young carers for

---

1   www.youngstonewall.org.uk

a weekly juice and biscuits and board games/chat meet-up and invite your local young carers association to come and speak.

- Wellbeing space: an MHFA will run mindfulness sessions every Thursday, for example.

Teacher referral

Training in this session is important because you want to get away from the culture of everyone just passing on to the safeguarding team or MHFA as a default response. Encourage every staff member to realize that mental health is everybody's business, and often the tutor or trusted teacher will be the best person to have that first conversation. We need to remind staff to see it as an honour and privilege and not a chore to support a young person through a difficult stage in their life. We entered the education profession because we are committed to supporting the whole child, not just their academic pathway.

Part 4: Training in day-to-day strategies and providing one-to-one support

In this training session you want to tackle academic expectations. An important consideration when supporting any student with mental health challenges is about ensuring that the school, the student and their parents all have realistic academic expectations.

Expecting a child to achieve beyond what they are currently capable of due to their psychological or physical wellbeing or following a period of absence can result in the student failing to live up to their expectations, which can feed into their anxieties and harmful behaviours.

Our mental wellbeing is linked to our academic results, and we need to ensure that as a society we don't neglect the first in pursuing the second.

In this session you will look at:

- Identifying triggers in the classroom.

- Resetting target grades (sometimes young people feel an inordinate amount of pressure to meet their high expected targets and a sense of overwhelming and looming failure before they have even begun).

- Additional support and tutoring.

- Removing stressful responsibilities and commitments (common amongst high achievers).

- Managing extracurricular activities, engaging the young person in extracurricular activities that will help them manage their stress or perhaps removing some extracurricular activities if they are over-committed.

- A reduced timetable, offering the young person safe places to go and slowly build up their resilience.

- Managing the use of safe spaces in a lesson and encouraging each student to have a plan that they use when in these spaces to help them calm down: breathing, reading, listening to music, drawing.

In the training session you will also want to look at specific one-to-one support that could be delivered by the MHFA or trained support staff.

This session should always be delivered alongside the individual student support mental wellbeing plan (see Appendix 5). This plan will include:

- The nature of the need.

- The programme and person they will be working with.

- The strategies identified to support the young person.

- Time-bound sessions and goals.

- Outcomes and impact.

Risk assessments: Often a risk assessment has to be completed on a child who is at risk, for example, of self-harming. For subjects like Food Prep and Textiles a risk assessment needs to be completed. It is important that a conversation is had with the student about what is self-harm and the different types of self-harm, and that they acknowledge their type of self-harm and the feelings connected with it, ensuring that they are allowed time to think through strategies for coping when they feel the urge to self-harm. This all needs to be put into the risk assessment. As an inclusive school you cannot exclude a young person from taking part in all lessons, but with a thorough risk assessment and a conversation with the young person in question, strategies can be put in place for coping when they feel the urge to self-harm.

This is a crucial piece of information because information needs to be clearly shared so that all key stakeholders know what they are doing.

One-to-one interventions should be time-bound and planned for a series of weeks, and could be for:

- Self-esteem and confidence-building programmes.

- An opportunity to explore and develop problem-solving skills.

- Setting up specific support programmes with mental health support teams related to anxiety, grief, trauma, eating disorders, substance misuse etc.

- Guidance, advice and information on where they can get further support.

- If necessary, conversations with parents and a referral to CAMHS.

Adult mental wellbeing mentors are generally trained MHFAs, and will be able to discuss with the students and their parents the appropriate support to ensure that the student keeps attending school and is able to feel safe enough to remain motivated and confident enough to stay focused on their learning. The MHFA and DMHL should also aim to work in collaboration with the SENCo and pastoral support teams, sharing information and providing students with reasonable adjustments.

Regarding what to actually do in the different types of interventions, I have provided a Recommended Reading List at the end of the book for different types of mental health challenges, all of which provide practical ideas for what to do. We need to remind ourselves here that the DMHL and MHFA must not try and replace the clinician. Our role is to listen with empathy and understanding and without judgement, and to find strategies to get the young person to talk about how they are feeling, identifying their triggers, and for them to come up with solutions and strategies – this is called non-directive therapy. For example, if you are working with a young person who is showing signs of self-harm and eating disorders, you could read *Self-Harm and Eating Disorders in Schools* by Dr Pooky Knightsmith.[2] Here she shares practical ideas for support:

- Play-Doh®, colours, drawing.

- Developing new ways to express emotions, such as journaling, art or poetry.

- Getting the students to generate a list of ideas of things they can do when they feel like self-harming.

- Exploring alternative ways to vent feelings; expressing they are feeling alone or down; to make them feel in control; doing a series of delay tactics to give them a short time to think.

In addition to reading up on the wealth of resources out there I also suggest using the NHS Every mind Matters - Mental Health advice - it covers all the most common mild to moderate mental health changes facing young people with practical suggestions and advice.

Contacting parents is also essential. School pastoral leads and mental wellbeing coordinators must not make any decision without consulting parents and students. They are key because if they don't have buy-in to your intervention programme, then it is very top-down and prescriptive.

---

2   Knightsmith, P. (2015) *Self-Harm and Eating Disorders in Schools: A Guide to Whole-School Strategies and Practical Support*. London: Jessica Kingsley Publishers.

Interventions on self-compassion and the concept of love (this could coincide with Valentine's Day)

These are some exercises for staff and students created by Sue Webb, Executive Consultant at Lotus Education.[3]

SELF-COMPASSION EXERCISE 1: HOW WOULD YOU TREAT A FRIEND?

Please take a sheet of paper and answer the following questions:

- First, think about times when a close friend feels bad about him or herself or is really struggling in some way. How would you respond to your friend in this situation? Please write down what you typically do, what you say, and note the tone in which you typically talk to your friends.

- Now think about times when you feel bad about yourself or are struggling. How do you typically respond to yourself in these situations? Please write down what you typically do, what you say, and note the tone in which you talk to yourself.

    Did you notice a difference? If so, ask yourself why. What factors or fears come into play that lead you to treat yourself and others so differently?

- Write down how you think things might change if you responded to yourself in the same way you typically respond to a close friend when you're suffering.

- Why not try treating yourself like a good friend and see what happens?

SELF-COMPASSION EXERCISE 2: IDENTIFYING WHAT WE REALLY WANT

- Think about the ways that you use self-criticism as a motivator. Is there any personal trait that you criticize yourself for having (too overweight, too lazy, too impulsive, etc.) because you think being hard on yourself will help you change? If so, first try to get in touch with the emotional pain that your self-criticism causes, giving yourself compassion for the experience of feeling so judged.

- Next, see if you can think of a kinder, more caring way to motivate yourself to make a change if needed. What language would a wise and nurturing friend, parent, teacher or mentor use to gently point out how your behaviour is unproductive, whilst simultaneously encouraging you to do something different? What is the most supportive message you can think of that's in line with your underlying wish to be healthy and happy?

- Every time you catch yourself being judgemental about your unwanted

---

3   https://lotuseducation.co.uk

trait in the future, first notice the pain of your self-judgement and give yourself compassion. Then try to reframe your inner dialogue so that it is more encouraging and supportive. Remember that if you really want to motivate yourself, love is more powerful than fear.

Supporting vulnerable students before the holidays start

Dr Pooky Knightsmith wrote a great article in SecEd about exactly this.[4] She advises:

- Schools getting the young person talking and thinking about the holidays.

- That the teacher or DMHL listens and understands how it feels from the student's perspective, working with them to problem-solve their anxiety, talking about who will know about their issues when they are at home in the holidays and to think about who can help.

- Discussing this with the young person and highlighting safe sources of online support.

- Encouraging a young person to carry a helpline number with them and developing a routine with them.

- Getting the young person thinking about their healthy coping mechanisms. This could be in a very practical way, literally making a box full of things the young person can go through in times of crisis, or a visual daily plan that splits the day into clear chunks – this can be invaluable in helping a young person manage their day.

Part 5: Delivering effective mental health lessons in the curriculum and ensuring the environment is safe

This training session ensures staff are familiar with the safeguarding policy and always keep in mind the needs of the most vulnerable student, allowing them to feed in before and after the lesson in a safe environment.

Delivering an effective mental health lesson is about:

- Preparation.

- Protection.

- Education.

---

4 Knightsmith, P. (2017) 'How to help vulnerable pupils prepare for the summer holidays.' SecEd, 7 June. Available at: www.sec-ed.co.uk/best-practice/how-to-help-vulnerable-pupils-prepare-for-the-summer-holidays

- Removing it from the first person to the third person.

- Signpost support where they can get help.

Preparation

Prepare for any eventuality. Think about who your target audience is. Always keep in mind: what could happen? You might get a disclosure. Don't see it as a negative; see this as a positive.

The lesson might trigger behaviours, so keep in mind how to protect against giving the young person ideas.

Protection

There are several things we can do when it comes to supporting vulnerable young people:

- Make your class aware of difficult topics.

- Make staff and parents aware – if staff know something about a student and they know what is coming up in the curriculum, they may be able to let relevant people know about a student.

- Invite input from students – have an 'Ask it' basket or a 'worry monster' – they may want to ask something but want to ask it anonymously. Make them feel supported.

- Finally, where we know there are students who are vulnerable, we need to stress that *they don't have to participate in discussions*; they can just listen. This is for students who we know may struggle. Students should have the 'right not to want to respond' if they don't want to answer any questions or take part in discussions. We can't plan for everything, but we can think ahead.

Education

Always review the lesson and look at it first before you share it with students. You may find additional videos and resources you want to use (which is great), but please review and check that it seeks to educate and there is no reference to 'how to'. We are here to educate and not instruct. Examine the information carefully and try and ensure it does not appear a 'how-to guide' like 'how to self-harm'.

Remove it from first person to third person

Keep it safe and sensitive and explore the topic in the third person. It can be awkward and uncomfortable and sometimes too close to home if explored in the first person. This also helps disclosures not happening in class but rather afterwards.

Videos and case studies are good ways of finding out about someone – a 'day in the life' perspective. Think about what that person might do. See it through someone else's eyes and not through the student's.

Make sure names are not used in class that have the same names as students in your class. This can have very embarrassing consequences for a child who gets embarrassed easily or where the mental health challenge seems to fit the student in the class.

Signpost support where they can get help.

Make sure you know Childline[5] and Samaritans[6] as these are excellent helplines to recommend to students. They are completely anonymous.

Discuss the benefits of accessing support.

In addition, The Mix has a free, confidential telephone helpline and online service that aims to find you the best help, whatever the problem. Shout 85258 provides free, confidential, 24/7 text message support in the UK for anyone struggling to cope. They can help with issues including suicidal thoughts, depression, anxiety, panic attacks, abuse, self-harm, relationship problems and bullying. Text "Shout" to 85258 to speak to an empathetic, trained volunteer who will listen and work with you to solve problems.

Finally, and this is very important to stress – explain what will happen next. Be honest. Be clear up front about having to contact parents and telling other teachers.

Ideas for mental health briefings

These are 10-minute briefings that can happen during the week before school. If you plan one every half term and six in total, you can really bring to attention anything urgent for all staff. In 10 minutes you simply cover:

What is it? Who does it affect? What are the signs? What should you (the educator) be doing or not doing?

Here are some topic ideas:

---

5   www.childline.org.uk
6   www.samaritans.org

- Suicide ideation: the safety plan and spotlighting male mental health that also crops up again later in the year with 'Movember', where there is a big campaign to look at mental health through a male lens.

- Supporting young people with complex behavioural needs. Support and de-escalation classroom strategies that are therapeutic and trauma-informed.

- Self-harm and risk assessments for students in the school.

- Eating disorders: how to support and signs to look out for.

- Managing panic attacks and supporting students with growing anxiety: what every teacher can say and do.

- How to incorporate 1-minute mindfulness and grounded breathing in your school day.

- Staff mental health and wellbeing: #teacher5aday.[7]

---

7   https://martynreah.wordpress.com/2014/12/06/teacher5aday

A–Z of Suggested Wellbeing Actions to Ensure Self-Care and Nurture

A–Z	Self-care at school	Self-care at home
A	Anxiety: what are the signs you show when you are anxious? What are the strategies you can have for dealing with them? Write it in your planner.	Awareness: take time to just be in the present and not to worry about yesterday or tomorrow. Have a mindful walk, mindful meditation. Unclutter your mind and have check-in points in the day and just enjoy the present.
B	Breathing: practise your grounded breathing before each lesson and at the end of each lesson.	Bake something sumptuous for a family member or with a family member. Enjoy the art of cooking, baking and giving.
C	Create spaces: in your classroom and office, for nature, calm, inspiration.	Connect with family and friends. Make time to listen and be in the present with them.
D	Difficult conversations. Don't let things fester. Have them – it will vastly improve your working relationship with students, colleagues and parents. Remain calm and explain how you feel and what the problem is. Listen and invite the other person to share their side of the story. Plan a way forward. Stay positive.	Dream of where you want to be in five years' time and plan your route and what you need to do. Identify your obstacles and challenges. Dream big – dreams do come true.
E	Eating: plan your lunch at school carefully. Aim for a balanced diet. Factor in that need for energy boost at the end of the school day.	Exercise: download the app and start 'Couch to 5K'[1] or sign up to a regular yoga or gym class. Aim for three times a week for at least 30 minutes a day.
F	Friendships in schools are precious. Nurture those friendships by making time for a cup of tea, random acts of kindness, saying thank you for the small things.	'Family mental health 5 a day' (#familyMH5aday) is about living the GREAT values and helping your family have a lifestyle shift: G = Give R = Relate E = Energize A = Awareness T = Try something new.[2]
G	Gossip: stay away from it.	Give some time up for a family member to do something they want. (See GREAT values above.)

---

1   www.nhs.uk/live-well/exercise/couch-to-5k-week-by-week
2   Watch this TEDx talk I did with my daughter on it at: www.youtube.com/watch?v=c5tuaUFyQrE

A–Z	Self-care at school	Self-care at home
H	Humour: it is vital to have a sense of humour and to see the light side of it all.	Hug someone.
I	Imposter syndrome: recognize it and deal with it by nipping those gremlins in the bud. Get on with the task at hand. You can do it.	Invite friends or family round at the weekend. Entertain. Have some friendship time.
J	Joke: joke with the kids. There is a fine line between negative sarcasm and a gentle joking environment – have a laugh with the kids and not at them. It will do wonders for your relationships.	Journal writing: encourage either morning intentions or evening reflections.
K	Kindness: model kindness and encourage a culture of kindness in your school from all stakeholders.	Know you are loved and love back. Keep the people you love your main priority – they always come first.
L	Lunch break: take a full lunch break on your own somewhere quiet at least three times a week.	Laugh: phone a friend, read a book, play with your kids, watch a comedy together. Laugh and try and take yourself less seriously.
M	Mindfulness: learn to do the 1-minute grounded breath and build up to 5 and then 10 minutes. Run sessions for staff and students to practise too.	Music: listen to your favourite music, dance to your favourite music, learn to play an instrument. Fill your life with music that calms and grounds you.
N	No: your 'no' means no and your 'yes' means yes. You know your limits.	Nibbles: cut out unhealthy ones and replace with fruit and veg.
O	Outdoor learning: explore ways you can take the lesson outside. Use the outdoor landscape as your teaching resource. Being surrounded by nature really helps the young people and teachers with improving mental wellbeing.	Opportunities: these will come and you may feel imposter syndrome (feelings and thoughts of inadequacy and self-doubt, often linked to a lack of confidence when doing something and comparing yourself to others). Keep trying new opportunities for learning about yourself and others. Broaden your out-of-school interests. Keep learning.
P	Plan your week before you start it. Know your lessons in advance and get the resources ready. The week will fly by with ease.	Plant seeds or bulbs in your garden. If you have a flat, get some pots. Bring some of your seeds into your classroom. Surround yourself with greenery and growth where possible. Bring the outdoors inside.
Q	Quiet: if your school has a staff wellbeing room, go and sit in it for some quiet time where you can practise 5-minute mindfulness. This will help you recharge and tune in to how you are feeling.	Quit: quit any bad habits such as smoking to eating too much junk food and heavy drinking to staying up late on digital technology.
R	Relationships: it's all about building relationships in the school setting. Even if a student is showing behavioural challenges, it's about reflecting and building on that relationship. Even if a colleague is being a bit difficult, always regard people as having the best intentions. See the positive.	Resilience: this is about reaching out for help and support when you feel you are struggling. Know who you can go to and where and when you can go to get the support you need. It's okay to not be okay. You can pull through with support.

A–Z	Self-care at school	Self-care at home
S	Successful heroes and sheroes: follow these people on social media. Surround yourself with people who inspire you.	Sleep: build in a nurturing sleep routine that helps you wind down and not think about school (reading, bathing, sleep meditations).
T	Tea: aim for antioxidant tea like green tea or rooibos. I have found these keep me calm and focused and, of course, hydrated.	Technology: treat as an asset to enable better engagement and efficiency. Beware of the addiction. Turn off when you can.
U	Understand that everyone has the best of intentions. Be mindful when you speak that you are supporting and respecting each other.	Unplug from digital technology. Get the whole family to do this. Have quality family time at the weekends.
V	Variety is the spice of life. Doing many different things, or often changing what you do makes life more interesting, and possibly even your lessons. Try different things. Keep learning.	Variety is the spice of life. Doing many different things, or often changing what you do, makes life more interesting. Try different things. Keep learning.
W	Water: drink regularly. Keep a filled-up bottle next to your desk. Drink at the end and start of each class.	Watch something light with the family on the TV or at the cinema.
X	Xenial means hospitable – be xenial to your students and colleagues. Host them with warmth and grace in your lessons and meetings.	Xanadu is an idealized place of great or idyllic magnificence and beauty – find your Xanadu in your home, hometown, a local walk or cycle. We are blessed with natural beauty all around us. We need to be able to look and appreciate it.
Y	Yes: your 'no' means no and your 'yes' means yes. If you say you are going to do something, then try and honour it, although know your limits. Be careful of what you sign up to, otherwise you will end up with too much on your plate.	Yes: your 'no' means no and your 'yes' means yes. If you say you are going to do something, then try and honour it, although know your limits. Be careful of what you sign up to, otherwise you will end up with too much on your plate.
Z	Zeal: do everything with zeal. Students and colleagues will feed off it. Your interests and passion will inspire others.	Zen – find your Zen when at home that is calm and peaceful. Experience it once a day.

Suggested Outcomes for Measuring the Impact of Interventions

These outcomes are courtesy of east to west,[1] a charity I had experience of working with. They are a fantastic organization that selflessly work with young people and their families struggling with difficult and damaging issues, from self-harming and bullying to broken family relationships, abuse and even homelessness. Most of their work takes place in schools with their relational support workers journeying alongside young people to understand their situations, grow their confidence and help them thrive. Based on all their years of experience, they have developed this set of outcomes to measure impact by, and I have found them to be extremely useful.

Anger management

1. Recognize anger triggers.

2. Able to recognize and monitor anger piling up.

3. Able to make positive choices when angry.

4. Less disruptive behaviour in class.

5. Less time out of class.

6. Reduced negative involvement of SLT and pastoral leaders.

7. Plateaued negative behavioural points or increased achievement points.

8. Engaging better with education: attendance, in class all lesson, participation and grades.

9. Improved relationship with teaching staff.

10. Improved social interaction.

---

1   www.easttowest.org.uk/what-we-do

Anxiety

1. Recognize emotional and physical trigger factors.

2. Increased awareness of stress or anxiety.

3. Able to self-monitor the build-up of stress or anxiety.

4. Increased ability to engage appropriate coping strategy.

5. Reduction in physical responses to stress, for example fewer or no panic attacks, or sleeping pattern improves.

6. Able to cope with challenging situations without catastrophizing.

7. Able to actively engage in a positive thinking cycle.

8. In school more, that is, less 'lates' or leaving early due to stress or anxiety recorded.

9. Engaging better with education: attendance, in class all lesson, participation and grades.

10. Exam completion.

11. Increased self-worth, how they see, carry and think about themselves.

12. Improved confidence in social and relational activity.

Behaviour

1. Increased knowledge of the consequences of actions or choices.

2. Willingness to change or adapt behaviour.

3. Increased usage of control mechanisms such as breathing or counting to 10.

4. Increased ability to make good choices.

5. Ability to assess situations for negative influences of behaviour, for example, a naughty friend in class.

6. Able to react well to problems and use appropriate strategies.

7. Reduced report or off report.

8. Engaging better with education: attendance, in class all lesson, participation and grades.

9. Improved relationship with teaching staff.

10. Improved relationships with peers.

11. Making a positive contribution to class.

Bullying/be bullied: Recognition of reasons why they may be bullied

1. Ability to seek appropriate help prior to things escalating.

2. Build a support network amongst peers.

3. Able to recognize victim mentality.

4. Increased self-worth through understanding role of boundaries.

5. Increased self-esteem, how they see, carry and think about themselves.

6. Increased self-confidence to use conflict resolution.

7. Ability to create boundaries and keep to them.

8. Bullying stopped.

9. Sticking up for others who are being bullied.

10. Engaging better with education: attendance, in class all lesson, participation and grades.

11. Implementing conflict resolution techniques more successfully.

Domestic violence
Child is the *object* of domestic violence

1. Speaking out about what is happening at home.

2. Child engaging with safeguarding lead and school process.

Child is a *witness* of domestic violence

1. Child is able to tell their story.

2. Child engages with safeguarding lead and school process.

3. Child engages with specialist support such as CAMHS.

4. Child is managing their response to emotions.

5. Able to create boundaries and keep to them.

6. Increased self-worth, how they see, carry and think about themselves.

Depression

1. Referral to CAMHS or doctor if required.

2. Able to self-monitor the build-up of depression.

3. Able to identify reasons behind emotions.

4. Application of strategies.

5. Able to feel happy emotions.

6. Reduction in low mood or sleeping improves or eats regular meals.

7. Able to see good in situations and people.

8. Engaging with change of negative thinking cycle.

9. Increased self-worth, how they see, carry and think about themselves.

10. Engaging better with education: attendance, in class all lesson, participation and grades.

11. Improved engagement in social and physical activity.

E-safety

1. Child engaging with safeguarding lead and school process.

2. Reduction in risky behaviour.

3. Awareness of own online identity and how to protect self-identity.

4. Awareness of others' online identities and risk of e-relationships.

5. Awareness of radicalization.

6. Awareness of longevity of information and images.

7. knowledge of dangers of accessing inappropriate material.

8. Aware of and using reporting and/or blocking mechanisms.

9. Increased knowledge of appropriate use of images.

10. Increased knowledge of the law and possible impact on themselves.

11. Able to discern coercive controlling behaviour in e-relationships.

12. Awareness of the increased dangers when moving from online to face-to-face.

13. Able to describe unhealthy effects of pornography.

14. Encourages and supports e-safety in others.

Family

1. Able to recognize and accept place in family.

2. Increased understanding of healthy relationships.

3. Able to protect self in dysfunctional relationships.

4. Improved relationships with family members.

5. Improved communication skills.

6. Implementing conflict resolution techniques more successfully.

7. Steps taken to begin restorative process with estranged family member/s.

Parents

1. Parents engaging with the support offered by school.

2. Parents engaging with outside agencies (such as a parenting course).

3. Empowering the parent to improve on their own low education (for example, English lessons).

Friendships

1. Increased knowledge of what a healthy friendship is.

2. Recognizing diversity within relationships.

3. Increased communication, able to say 'no' or disagree comfortably.

4. Able to manage other people's emotional responses.

5. Able to create boundaries and keep to them.

6. Increased ability to form better and new friendships.

7. Increased self-worth, how they see, carry and think about themselves.

8. Improved ability to resolve conflicts.

9. Reduced need for staff involvement.

10. Happier break and lunchtimes.

11. Able to build resilience and grow despite friendship instability.

12. Engaging better with education: attendance, in class all lesson, participation and grades.

Grief
Bereavement, divorce and/or separation

1. Describe and apply grief or loss process.

2. Allowing themselves to experience the stages of grief model.

3. Better handling of the process of loss or grief, less breaking down, able to talk about life.

4. Demonstrating courage to allow life to impact their situation.

5. Doing new things and building resilience.

6. Able to display a healthy release of emotions.

7. Adapting to new family roles.

8. Engaging better with education: attendance, in class all lesson, participation and grades.

9. Ability to describe how they are feeling.

10. Able to hold positive memories and celebrate what was before the loss.

Homelessness
Homeless or temporary parental estrangement

1. Able to express the breakdown process that led to being homeless or kicked out.

2. Child engaging with safeguarding lead and school process.

3. Reduction in risky behaviour.

4. Knowledge of support services such as food bank.

5. Engaging better with education: attendance, in class all lesson, participation and grades.

6. Involvement with social services or housing services.

7. Improved hygiene.

8. Restoration or reconciliation process begun.

Looked after child

1. Security of placement.

2. Demonstrates understanding of self-identity.

3. Able to pinpoint areas of growth and development in self-identity.

4. Able to recognize and accept place in family.

5. Able to protect self in dysfunctional relationships.

6. Improved or renewed relationships with family members.

7. Improved communication skills.

8. Implementing conflict resolution skills more successfully.

9. Increased self-worth, how they see, carry and think about themselves.

10. Able to establish relationship and maintain with significant other adult or member of staff.

Pregnant

1. Engaging in informed decision-making and receiving advice for future.

2. Family or safe adult support through decision-making.

3. Sexual health check or attends medical clinic.

4. Engaging with pre-natal services or attending post-abortion services.

5. Engaging better with education: attendance, in class all lesson, participation and grades.

6. Reduction in risky behaviour.

7. Attending to sexual health.

Self-esteem

1. Increased self-worth, how they see, carry and think about themselves.

2. Identify themselves as unique.

3. Healthy friendship or relational engagement.

4. Engaging better with education: attendance, in class all lesson, participation and grades.

5. Engaging better at home.

6. Improved relationships in all aspects of life.

7. Increased confidence.

8. Engages in extracurricular activity.

Self-harm

1. Young person engages with safeguarding lead and school process.

2. Has told home or is beginning to open up about self-harm.

3. Able to describe health hazards of open wounding or other forms of self-harm.

4. Recognizes emotional and physical trigger factors.

5. Reduces self-harming episodes.

6. Able to engage with healthier coping strategies.

7. Stopped self-harming.

8. Increased self-worth, how they see, carry and think about themselves.

9. Increased ability to form better and new friendships or relationships at home.

Sexual health

1. Child engages with safeguarding lead and school process.

2. Reduction in risky behaviour.

3. Knowledge of healthy relationships.

4. Able to discern coercive controlling behaviour and its potential impact.

5. Able to explain unhealthy effects of pornography.

6. Able to apply healthy boundaries within relationships.

7. Able to keep sexual relationship in healthy context.

8. Displays knowledge of contraception and its place in safer sex.

9. Accessing medical support (genitourinary medicine (GUM), GP, pharmacy etc.).

10. Being able to share corporate responsibility (with parent or partner).

11. Demonstrates broader impact of sexual relationship on overall wellbeing.

Sexuality

1. Displays confidence in exploring their sexuality.

2. Accessing specialist agencies from gendered intelligence to online forums offering support to young people around sexual identity.

3. Knowledge of healthy relationships in all areas.

4. Able to discern coercive controlling behaviour and its potential harm.

5. Able to create boundaries and keep to them.

6. Able to involve family or seek consistent support from safe adult.

7. Knowledge of the process of acceptance of their sexuality by others.

8. Displays knowledge of broader impact of sexuality on overall wellbeing.

Sexual assault or rape

1. Speaking out about what has happened.

2. Child engaging with safeguarding lead and school process.

3. Cooperating with appropriate authorities.

4. Accessing specialist survivor support via independent sexual violence adviser or independent domestic violence adviser.

5. Accessing medical support (from genitourinary medicine (GUM), GP, pharmacy, family planning).

6. Support child survivor through police process or court case.

7. Child managing their response to emotions.

8. Restored loss of confidence.

9. Engaging better with education: attendance, in class all lesson, participation and grades.

10. Able to hold the rape crime in context and continue with healthy relational engagement.

Substance abuse
Child is *user*

1. Child engaging with safeguarding lead and school process.

2. Recognition of triggers and root of use.

3. Able to explain negative effects of substance abuse.

4. Able to explain effects of behaviour on others.

5. Increased ability to take personal responsibility to change.

6. Accessing appropriate medical support (GP, pharmacy).

7. Accessing specialist support agencies, for example, Catch 22.[2]

8. Change in substance use.

9. Healthier physically.

10. Healthier lifestyle.

11. Reduction in criminal activity or associated risky behaviour.

12. Engaging better with education: attendance, in class all lesson, participation and grades.

13. Stops substance abuse.

Substance abuse, living with
Child is *living with* substance abuse

1. Speaking out about what is going on at home.

2. Able to separate behaviour dominated by substance.

3. Able to recognize root of their anxiety.

4. Able to build resilience and grow despite unstable home environment.

---

2   www.catch-22.org.uk

5. Accessing specialist support agencies.

6. Developing relationship of significant other or supportive network.

Young carer

1. Recognizing the process.

2. Ability to talk through how they are feeling.

3. Able to hold positive memories and celebrate what was before the loss.

4. Improved teacher or trusted adult relationship.

5. Growing resilience to enable adjustment to take place.

6. Embraces change.

7. Settled behaviour.

8. Engaging better with education: attendance, in class all lesson, participation and grades.

9. New friendships formed.

Note: I came across these from a charity called east to west,[3] which supplies relational support workers alongside young people to understand their situations, grow their confidence and help them thrive. Their work takes place in one-to-one and group sessions, listening to and caring for students over several months or even years. Over the years I have adapted these outcomes, but what I liked was that they put each category in coloured boxes, laminated them and made them into a keyring-style flip resource to quickly refer to when setting up mental health intervention outcomes. I am delighted they have allowed me to share these with the reader.

---

3   www.easttowest.org.uk/what-we-do

Pre-emptive Mental Health and Wellbeing Concern Flowchart

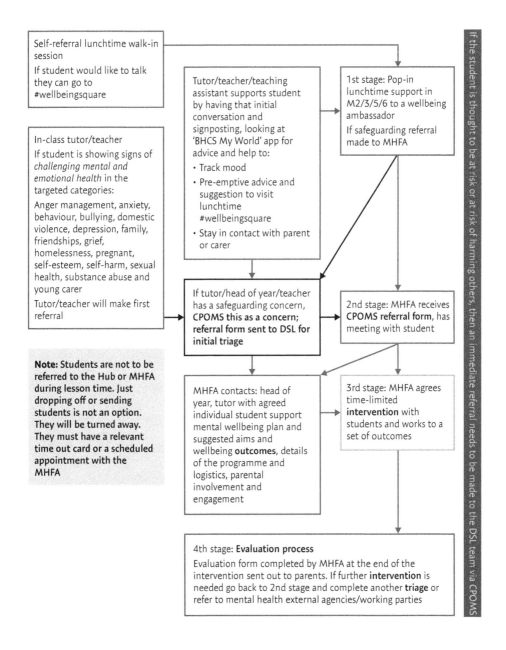

Self-referral lunchtime walk-in session

If student would like to talk they can go to #wellbeingsquare

In-class tutor/teacher

If student is showing signs of *challenging mental and emotional health* in the targeted categories:

Anger management, anxiety, behaviour, bullying, domestic violence, depression, family, friendships, grief, homelessness, pregnant, self-esteem, self-harm, sexual health, substance abuse and young carer

Tutor/teacher will make first referral

Note: Students are not to be referred to the Hub or MHFA during lesson time. Just dropping off or sending students is not an option. They will be turned away. They must have a relevant time out card or a scheduled appointment with the MHFA

Tutor/teacher/teaching assistant supports student by having that initial conversation and signposting, looking at 'BHCS My World' app for advice and help to:

• Track mood
• Pre-emptive advice and suggestion to visit lunchtime #wellbeingsquare
• Stay in contact with parent or carer

1st stage: Pop-in lunchtime support in M2/3/5/6 to a wellbeing ambassador

If safeguarding referral made to MHFA

If tutor/head of year/teacher has a safeguarding concern, **CPOMS this as a concern; referral form sent to DSL for initial triage**

2nd stage: MHFA receives **CPOMS referral form**, has meeting with student

MHFA contacts: head of year, tutor with agreed individual student support mental wellbeing plan and suggested aims and wellbeing **outcomes**, details of the programme and logistics, parental involvement and engagement

3rd stage: MHFA agrees time-limited **intervention** with students and works to a set of outcomes

4th stage: **Evaluation process**

Evaluation form completed by MHFA at the end of the intervention sent out to parents. If further **intervention** is needed go back to 2nd stage and complete another **triage** or refer to mental health external agencies/working parties

If the student is thought to be at risk or at risk of harming others, then an immediate referral needs to be made to the DSL team via CPOMS

The #wellbeingsquare is made up of:

M2 – Freedom 2B space

M3 – Q space

M4 – Pop-in anti-bullying space to talk to an anti-bullying ambassador

M5 – YC space (young carers)

M6 – Wellbeing space

Hub – For one-to-one appointment (referrals first made to DSL) with **mental health first aider (MHFA)**

Individual Student Support Mental Wellbeing Plan

Important points to consider:

- It is not our place to diagnose the student with any condition. It is our place to be pre-emptive and proactive. CAMHS and the GP diagnose.

- Ensure all forms are kept in the student's file for evidence in case a referral needs to be made.

- We are not a counselling service. Instead, we offer non-directive therapy (listening with empathy, offering support and signposting, helping the student to problem-solve for themselves). Where possible we bring in expert agencies with specialized skills.

Generic Student Support Mental Wellbeing Internal Referral Form

Date:

Referred by:

Student name:

SEN: PP: Y/N   On CP Reg: Y/N   Y/Carer: Y/N   FSM: Y/N[1]

Attendance %:   Behaviour points: Achievement points:

Is parent or carer aware of referral?

Have you had a conversation with parent or carer?

What interventions have been implemented so far? (Please highlight)

Tutee mentoring

Tutor report

---

[1]   SEN = special educational needs; PP = Pupil Premium; CP Reg = Child Protection Register; Y/Carer = young carer; FSM = free school meals.

Pop-in lunchtime spaces in #wellbeingsquare

Reason for referral/issues/concerns:

- ☐ Anger
- ☐ Bully or bullying
- ☐ Bereavement
- ☐ Family
- ☐ OCD behaviour
- ☐ Self-harm
- ☐ Young carer
- ☐ Anxiety
- ☐ Depression
- ☐ Eating disorders
- ☐ Friendships
- ☐ Self-esteem (low)
- ☐ Substance misuse
- ☐ Other

Please specify: _____

Do you think they would benefit from:

- ☐ Group work intervention?
- ☐ One-to-one sessions?
- ☐ Same-sex mentor?
- ☐ Extracurricular styled intervention?

Any other relevant information: _____

Individual Student Support Mental Wellbeing Plan

Has the tutor or head of year had a conversation with the parent?

What was the outcome?

Is the young person known to CAMHS?

Is the young person known to any other counselling service?

If so, which agency?

Are they known to our DSL?

Are they known to the SENCo?

What intervention would suit them best?

Who or what agency would be best to mentor the student?

What does the young person want from this referral?

Type of six-week intervention put into place?

What are the outcomes? (See Appendix 3.)

Engaging the Family in #familyMH5aday (Family Mental Health 5 a Day)

For a student wellbeing programme to work we need to connect parents with the work we are doing in school; we need parents' role modelling from the top – pushing for an environment at home that nurtures positive mental wellbeing. We need to encourage families to see mental wellbeing as the development of 'mental wealth'.

But let's be honest here – parents are the hardest audience to reach. Schools have limited contact, and it is difficult to lecture parents, as it may be perceived as interfering with their parenting, and they may have many different attitudes to wellbeing and mental health.

The #familyMH5aday campaign is something simple and easy to follow, adaptable, light-hearted, positive and fun. But it can have a real impact and enables parents to model behaviours that are crucial to reinforcing the work of the school. It's about getting the parents and carers, grandparents and siblings to come together, encouraging positive interaction with each other, and to take part in a range of activities that encourage real-time connection with each other and the world around them before digital time connection.

I launched the #familyMH5aday campaign in my own family unit and then through my school. It involves embracing five lifestyle concepts that promote positive mental wellbeing. I call them 'living the GREAT values':

G = Give

R = Relate

E = Energize

A = Awareness

T = Try something new.

You can find out more about this #familyMH5aday campaign in a TEDx talk[1] I did with my daughter on it. Its title is 'How to strengthen family relationships' by

---

[1]   www.ted.com/talks/rosie_and_claire_erasmus_strengthening_familiy_relationships_by_really_communicating_and_listening_familymh5aday

Rosie Erasmus and Clare Erasmus and I have included templates for you to use and adapt here as well.

Examples of #familyMH5aday activities

Want to have positive mental wellbeing as a family?

Embrace these GREAT values

Student activities: #familyMH5aday

Week	G = Give	R = Relate	E = Energize	A = Awareness	T = Try something new
1	Hug a friend, buddy or family member and tell them something special in person or start a Snapchat streak with them (1 HP).	Put your phone away or switch the TV off for one family dinner and have a conversation starting with 'How was your day?' (1 HP).	Go for a walk with your family, and take a family selfie (2 HP).	Go for a 30-minute walk and try not to look at your phone but be aware of the winter season and the five senses (3 HP).	Bake something seasonal, Christmas themed, with a family member or friend such as a gingerbread man and share with the family. Take a photo (3 HP).
2	Offer to wash the dishes after a family meal or stack or unstack the dishwasher (1 HP).	Interview family members talking about most embarrassing, scary or happiest moments (3 HP).	Create a 'gadget basket' and place your gadgets in there after an agreed time in the house, e.g. no electronic device an hour before bed (includes Xbox, PlayStation, phones, etc.) (3 HP).	Watch or listen to the headline news; note down if it changes during the day. Reflect on what is the biggest crisis in our world today (1 HP).	Make a Christmas card for a family member and take a photo (1 HP).
3	Before you get asked, offer to clean your bedroom (even if you share). Take a photo before and after (3 HP).	Write a thank you card to a teacher, parent or friend who helps you a lot. Give it to them (3 HP).	Lie down and read a non-digital book, magazine or newspaper and *relax* for 20 minutes (2 HP).	When you wake up, think of five things you are grateful for and text or email them to yourself or write them down or take a photo of what you are grateful for (2 HP).	Try to tell a new short, 'clean' joke to a family member or friend. Try to collect as many 'clean' jokes as you can for your tutor group and write a family or tutor joke book (3 HP).

4	Put together a Christmas essentials food box for the local food bank (2 HP).	Play a board game with a family member; don't cheat and congratulate the winner if you lose (3 HP).	Eat three different healthy breakfasts. Take photos of how different they were. Share the recipes (3 HP).	Download a Mindfulness app like HeadSpace[2] and try and do one relaxed breathing exercise a day (3 HP).	Take part in an inter-house activity. Get your tutor group to cheer you on. How did that feel? (2 HP)
5	As a family, put up the Christmas decorations and take four photographs of during and after, or talk about what are meaningful free gifts you can give to each other. Set yourself the challenge (4 HP).	Watch a favourite TV programme or film with a family member or friend and cook homemade popcorn. What was the film or TV programme? (3 HP)	Drink seven glasses of water for a day. What do you notice at the end of the day? Always carry a full water bottle with you (2 HP).	'Magic Moments'[3] – get yourself an envelope or jar to write on or store lovely experiences, such as time with family and friends, celebration days, personal experiences etc. When you are feeling anxious, open your 'Magic Moments' and check how great you are (3 HP).	Either play an instrument, board game or sport you have not played in a while or learn to play a new one. Try and involve one family member (3 HP).

Note: HP = house point.

Please sign each box after your child and/or family have successfully achieved each activity. Please also sign the pledge of authenticity at the bottom of this page.

_____

_____

_____

2   www.headspace.com
3   With thanks to Nina Jackson; see https://teachlearncreate.com/author/nina/page/2

Week	G = Give	R = Relate	E = Energize	A = Awareness	T = Try something new
	Want to have positive mental wellbeing as a family? **Embrace these GREAT values** **Parent activities: #familyMH5aday**				
1	Give someone else in the family a break from a chore they always or usually do. Take over the shopping, washing etc. for a day, the weekend or the festive season.	Aim to have five family meals without any gadgets, TV or phones and have a family conversation.	Go for a walk with your family, run or cycle, exploring a new area.	Go for an evening moonlit walk with some of your family. Notice the evening sky and how things are different from the day. Chat about the day.	Bake or cook something you haven't tried before with a family member – Christmas or seasonal themed – and share with the family. Take a photo.
2	Give yourself some 'Me time'. Let the family know so you are not interrupted but make sure you take 30 minutes out of the day just for you. Treat yourself.	Phone or Skype an older family member who lives away from you and who you have not spoken to for a while, and have a long conversation.	Turn off the Wi-Fi at meal times and before bed time, or just for an hour a day.	Watch or listen to the headline news; note down if it changes during the day. Reflect on what is the biggest crisis in our world today with your family over a dinner conversation.	Let your children try to teach you something. For example, get them to teach you Minecraft, a computer game, a new dance, a maths equation or a historical fact.
3	Find a charity event and either fundraise for it or host a 'fun' event for it. It could be any charity that is either topical for that month or that means something to you, e.g. 'Movember' or breast cancer.	Give each child some one-to-one time, doing something together for a set time with no disruptions. Possibly ask them open-ended questions about their school, friends, anxieties and dreams. Have fun together.	Lie down and read a non-digital book or magazine and *relax* for 30 minutes. Take a photo of what you were reading *or* give yourself a home pamper session *or* do both.	When you wake up, think of five things you are grateful for and text or email them to yourself or write them down or take a photo of what you are grateful for.	Take part in a hobby or activity that another family member or friend does.

4	Let your child see you doing something for someone else, e.g. helping a neighbour, grandparent, visiting a nursing or care home, making cakes for someone, showing you care for others.	Watch one YouTube video from Time to Change[4] about mental wellbeing. Discuss with a family member what it means to have positive mental wellbeing.	Eat three different healthy breakfasts and introduce healthy snacks into the house for the family to eat. Drink more water.	Write down what your most stressful points in the day are. Think about what you can do to de-stress the triggers. Different habits perhaps? Different approaches? Talk to your family if you need help.	Read a magazine or newspaper or non-fiction book you would not normally read. Finish it. Take a photo of the page you found most interesting.
5	Organize an alternative advent calendar where the kids are encouraged to put one thing into a box for homeless people or something for the food bank.	Play some games together with the family, go to the cinema and/ or let someone else in the family choose the DVD to watch.	Go out on the bikes with a sketch pad and draw something en route or take photos of striking scenes.	'Magic Moments'[5] – get yourself an envelope or jar to write on or store lovely experiences, such as time with family and friends, celebration days, personal experiences etc. When you are feeling anxious, open your 'Magic Moments' and check how great you are.	Go to a gig or concert in a music genre you wouldn't say you like. Likewise, buy a novel in a style you wouldn't normally choose. If you never usually go, go to the ballet or rugby. Just extend yourself and *live* ☺

4   www.time-to-change.org.uk
5   With thanks to Nina Jackson; see https://teachlearncreate.com/author/nina/page/2

'A comprehensive and most importantly, highly practical guide for Mental Health Leads from one of the UK's leading experts. An invaluable resource that deserves to be read widely, and revisited often.'

– *James Hilton, Wellbeing speaker and author of* Leading from the Edge

'Clare Erasmus is a trail blazer in supporting the mental health of both students and staff. This is a work book for the whole year as well as a much needed guide to the breadth of support available to schools. This is essential to aid recovery after Covid and this book is a much needed lifeline for both new and existing DMHLs.'

– *Vivienne Porritt, co-editor of* 10% Braver: Inspiring
Women to Lead Education *and* Being 10% Braver

'Through a passion to provide the most effective model to support all schools' mental health provision and grow a deeper understanding of what is required of all staff, not only the DMHL, this book outlines every necessary area we as leaders need to focus on. The step by step, well written, and easy-to-read guide is supported at every stage with concrete evidence derived from research and great practice.'

– *Christalla Jamil, Executive Headteacher of two inner London schools*

'Claire has a wealth of experience and expertise in mental health that this book captures to provide the perfect balance between operational and strategic guidance not only for DMHLs, but also for other senior leaders, headteachers and governors who take seriously the challenge of creating a culture of care, mental health and wellbeing in their schools.'

– *Patrick Ottley-O'Connor, Executive Headteacher*